Woodworking Tools and Accessories

A Complete Guide to Learning about Woodworking Tools, Preparing Your Woodshop, and Making Beautiful DIY Projects

MILES ADKINS

© Copyright 2021 by MILES ADKINS – All rights reserved

This document is geared towards providing exact and reliable information in regard to the topic and issue covered. The publication is sold with the idea that the publisher is not required to render accounting, officially permitted, or otherwise, qualified services. If advice is necessary, legal or professional, a practiced individual in the profession should be ordered.

From a Declaration of Principles which was accepted and approved equally by a Committee of the American Bar Association and a Committee of Publishers and Associations.

In no way is it legal to reproduce, duplicate, or transmit any part of this document in either electronic means or printed format. Recording of this publication is strictly prohibited and any storage of this document is not allowed unless with written permission from the publisher. All rights reserved.

The information provided herein is stated to be truthful and consistent, in that any liability, in terms of inattention or otherwise, by any usage or abuse of any policies, processes, or Instructions contained within is the solitary and utter responsibility of the recipient reader. Under no circumstances will any legal responsibility or blame be held against the publisher for any reparation, damages, or monetary loss due to the information herein, either directly or indirectly.

Respective authors own all copyrights not held by the publisher.

The information herein is offered for informational purposes solely and is universal as so. The presentation of the information is without a contract or any type of guarantee assurance.

The trademarks that are used are without any consent, and the publication of the trademark is without permission or backing by the trademark owner. All trademarks and brands within this book are for clarifying purposes only and are the property of the owners themselves, they are not affiliated with this document.

Table of Contents

Introduction	1
CHAPTER 1: What Is Woodworking	4
1.1 Woodworkers	4
1.2 Carvers	5
1.3 Furniture makers	5
1.4 Turners	5
1.5 Whittlers	5
1.6 Machine Setters	5
1.7 Framers	6
1.8 Carpenters	6
1.9 Construction Managers	6
1.10 Attributes of a Woodworker	7
1.11 Misconceptions about Woodworking	8
1.12 Why should children be taught woodworking?	12
CHAPTER 2: Evolution of Woodworking	16
2.1 Woodworking Advantages	29
2.2 Primitive Woodworking Tools Still in Use	30
2.3 Essential Information	34
CHAPTER 3: Learn to Use Woodworking Tools Every Woodworker Needs	36
3.1 Essential Woodworking Hand Tools	36
3.2 Make a Try Square	53

3.3 Get a Pair of Dividers (Compass)	54
3.4 Make a Marking Gauge	55
3.5 Get a Rabbet Plane	58
3.6 Power Tools every woodworker should have	64

CHAPTER 4: Woodworking Projects — 79

1. Cantilever End Table	79
2. Hexagonal Shelves	86
3. Wooden Key Hanger	90
4. Portable Laptop Stand	96

Chapter 5: Tips for Starting the Woodworking — 99

Start with What You Have	99
Buy Tools You Will Use Anyway	99
Start with Hand Tools before Power Tools	100
Initially Invest in Small Power Tools	100
Invest in Quality for Heavily Used Tools	100
Buy Tools and Supplies as and when Required	100
Measure Twice, Cut Once	101
Label Your Cut Parts as You Cut Them	101
Cut Pieces a Little Larger	101
Keep the Smallest Scraps of Wood	101
Keep Your Work Area Clean and Organized	102

Conclusion — 103

Introduction

Wood is an easily available material. Furthermore, it is an extremely workable material. Undoubtedly, it would have been one of the first things that human beings utilized to create shelters with the help of the simplest and easy-to-use tools. A wide range of tree species come in different grades and have to be dried properly before using it for conventional work. You can also get the wood without spending any money, especially if you recognize friendly landowners or tend to recycle old pieces. Anyway, it doesn't have to be expensive to get started. You have to stay away from the MDF as it contains toxic ingredients such as formaldehyde, and there are risks of health associated with it. So there are periods when using additional human-made resources such as plywood would make sense—making the box-type arrangements like kitchens, wardrobes, and other cabinetry is far more economical. In this situation, using solid wood is a tad of waste. You don't need a lot of knowledge, experience, and tools to start woodworking. Neither do you necessarily require a dedicated workshop. You can work outdoors for a large part of the year, but you require a dry space for storing your wood and work on something. A simple wood box or a bench could be one of the first projects as a beginner. Tools must be too sharp—enough for removing the hairs from your arm. When purchased, the tools don't get fully sharpened unless they're of too high quality. All these tools should come with a field bevel that must be polished with fine quality sharpening mortar. Several sharpening stones are available—like a ceramic diamond or water stones, and each has its fan. You may make a wooden toolbox for storing tools so that they won't get damaged. If you work outdoors, it is useful to have a plastic one. Even a conventional carpenter canvas bag can be easily carried and is handy too. If you're using the power tools, you'll need gloves, socks, dust covers, and ear protectors. Many people love woodworking as a hobby but don't think they can create a real profession. As a skilled woodworker, you can create and develop a range of items for companies or households, such as chairs, tables, and other structures. These are made of wood, veneers, and laminates. Woodworkers also incorporate different material styles into the wood to make some of the finest items around. Despite the abundance of metals, plastics, and other materials, wood products are still important in our lives. Woodworkers have the expertise and skills to produce products from timber and other wood products using their specifically learned and acquired skills. In the past, woodworkers were considered skilled in making delicate furniture by using their hands and other tools. Modern woodworkers are formally educated in the skills and skillfully use various kinds of machinery to complete their work. As a woodworker, you should be able to understand the drawings developed by architects. You should have rudimentary knowledge about setting up machines that will be used for woodwork manufacturing. Additionally, it would be best if you were willing to equip yourself with the advanced knowledge that is required for using woodworking machines. You should have sound knowledge of industry standards and other specifications to develop projects in compliance with the clients' specific requirements. Most importantly, you should have the expertise and skill to choose the right cutting, milling, boring, and sanding tools. Furthermore, you should be equipped with the basic working knowledge regarding the use of hand tools that play an important role in creating different projects. Several people who want to work with wood do not trust they have the patience or the ability to transform their interest into a profession. A quite commonly high school certificate is a key to being a woodworker. So, there are generally about three years dedicated to studying how to do a job skillfully. Many activities are performed on the job. Companies look for candidates that have advanced experiences in both programming and mathematics. By taking more courses at technical schools or community colleges, you as a woodworker gain extra talents. There are even universities offering degrees in wood technology, furniture fabrication, and manufacturing. These courses prepare students for engineering, management, manufacturing, and supervisory jobs. While there are numerous features to start with woodworking, understanding them is essential. Do you have the skills that the timber worker needs each day? Or perhaps you already have certain certifications in the back pockets? Consider the dreams and skills—once you've realized that woodworking is the area, and nothing can prevent you from becoming a professional worker of woodworking. This book is excellent for those interested in getting started in woodcrafts but have no idea where to start. It is equally good for those who feel overwhelmed by the idea of embarking on woodworking as a career. Read on and this book will provide you with a clear path to get you started.

CHAPTER 1:

What Is Woodworking

In woodworking, a woodworker creates objects using wood with the help of hand or power tools. Woodworking is simple yet extremely diverse, as it involves making simple projects from wall hanging to the development of an intricate and precise cabinet. People who create doors and windows and related items are called bench joiners and are typically workshop-oriented. A good woodworker knows how to get the most out of the various materials, from natural timber to plywood or strand board. It's not just about tool skills, but design and planning as well. Let us first briefly discuss the different types of woodworking-related skills and jobs, along with earning potential for a better understanding of this exciting field.

1.1 Woodworkers

By chopping, smoothing, arranging, shaping and preservation treatment, woodworkers convert wood into products. The sectors that employ woodworkers include furniture making, mobile home manufacture, and building. Their occupations are dependent on the economy. Construction activities rise when the conditions are favorable and so does the market for wood products. The woodworkers construct and design wood items such as boxes, cabinets, chairs, and musical tools. Hand tools like hammers, saws, and planes, or mechanical devices like routers, drill presses, and lathes may be used by the workers during the work. Loud noises, wounds, or cuts may harm them, and they necessarily wear protective clothing like goggles, gloves, and earplugs. They can even be unprotected from chemicals, pollutants, and dust that are hazardous. They can get training through formal traineeships or often through vocational schools and community colleges.

1.2 Carvers

In addition to functioning on flat surfaces, carvers typically work in free-standing ways. They're artists, and their medium is woodworking.

1.3 Furniture makers

This category of cabinet-making sometimes includes furniture makers. They make desks, cabinets, rocking chairs, tables, etc.

1.4 Turners

The Turners are a specialized collection of woodworkers who are skilled in lathe work. They also make plates, bowls, and all kinds of curved items.

1.5 Whittlers

In reality, these are people, typically hobbyists or amateurs, who chip out wood and carve small items. The best can create impressive objects, including chains, rests of books, containers, and all sorts of small trinkets.

1.6 Machine Setters

Special woodworking devices, including lathes, drill presses, saws, sanders, routers, and planers, are taught to machine setters. Workers need to be capable of setting up equipment, change options to suit job specifications, check sizes, and maintain the machines in a working manner. Employers are likely to educate those with a minimum diploma of high school because the machines used in the creation of products have become more advanced. Many with technical school qualifications could enhance their chances for employment. It is anticipated that employment will rise at higher rates than normal.

1.7 Framers

They are not typically regarded as artists because their function is to build a structure's roof, floors, and/or walls. When it comes to the structural integrity of a home, there isn't too much room for creative license.

1.8 Carpenters

The framework of the structures such as doors, windows, walls, stairs, and cabinets are erected and repaired by carpenters. Since they lift large pieces of stand, wood, kneel and execute repetitive actions, the task may be strenuous and physically challenging. Many work twenty-four-hour, including the evenings and weekends, and it is normal to work overtime. Almost 40 percent of them are freelancing. Usually, through official apprenticeships from the unions and employer organizations, carpenters learn their jobs. During the education, which usually lasts three to four years and involves professional and on-job aspects, they receive salaries.

1.9 Construction Managers

The woodworkers with several experience years will progress to become building general contractors or managers after having acquired administrative, budgeting, and operational skills. Through collaborating with the engineers and architects and hiring the construction workers like electricians, carpenters, and laborers, these professionals supervise construction projects. A bachelor's degree is typically necessary for architecture, construction science, or construction management, in addition to experience. For several months or years, fresh contractors typically serve as assistants to additional experienced supervisors. To complete projects, they often work long hours and may spend days in the construction sites and offices. Those managing many tasks would frequently travel.

1.10 Attributes of a Woodworker

An excellent way to make a woodworking career is by taking your projects online. This means sharing your projects as ideas for DIY projects through a blog format, selling your products, or simply sharing your hobby and earning some money. For the sake of being successful in woodworking, here are abilities absolutely compulsory to recognize and master. Most of the skills were once taught in the U.S. in high schools, but nowadays most woodshop classes are suspended, and people have to learn from the professionals or by trial and error through college classes, apprenticeships, and internships.

Woodworkers must have good hand and eye coordination for making detailed cuts; math and computer skills (particularly when working in the manufacturing) to the proper manufacture objects and furniture; machine adjustment and calibration skills; strength and physical stamina. They also need to be concerned with details and acquire the required professional expertise in understanding and translating sketches and manuals. In addition, woodworkers must have the working knowledge of all tools and how to use them with safety. A woodworker must get a full understanding of every project and its requirements. Moreover, a woodworker should be able to prepare and set up the machines. A good woodworker must apply and dedicate himself to acquiring knowledge of the several hand tools, hand drills, the drill press, drill bits, band saws, etc. He should have the necessary information about the different kinds of wood that would be needed for different DIY and more advanced projects. Finally, a woodworker should be able to give exquisite final touches to his products. This can be achieved only if he has a basic knowledge of numerous materials that were used in finishing, that is, stains, lacquers, varnishes, and glosses.

1.11 Misconceptions about Woodworking

Woodworking, as with any new-fangled hobby, can be a bit challenging in the beginning. Furthermore, there's also a lot of corrupted information about woodworking. Some misconceptions are as follows:

Woodworking Is Investment-Centric

The first misconception that usually decelerates new woodworkers is the fact that you might think it's costly to start. Again, it depends on what sort of woodworking you get into, but usually, there are lower rate options for even more costly woodworking types. Most small to standard size woodworking projects may be easy to manufacture and can be manufactured with hand tools. If you look for hand tools or look for second-hand tools, then you can also cut the start-up charges and still make a lot of amazing projects. We recommend you to look for your first few tools online in the market of second-hand. Take somebody with you who knows the tools, and they may check those before you buy them. Begin small. At first, you just need basic tools. You can improve more over time, and this is how you will end up having a lot of the tools.

A Great Number of Tools Are Required for Woodworking

One of the main misconceptions of going into woodworking is that there are multiple materials that you require to start as a woodworker. You don't, and you can typically start with a few and work up to get more. It depends on your project, but the purchase of very few tools can help you to get started on your woodworking projects. Smaller tasks, usually requiring only one tool, such as lathe work, appear to be on the less costly side, so you don't require many devices. If you're doing elaborate things, you can still reduce your number of tools if you're willing to use the same tools for different projects in a creative way. Small power devices like cordless drills can also be used.

Woodworking Is Very Demanding and Challenging

The third misconception about woodworking is that it is a very intricate activity and learning about woodworking requires a long time. Woodworking is a big field in general, therefore yes, it will take a long time to learn all of it. In fact, learning all of that could take numerous lifetimes. That said, you're not looking to learn everything about it from the onset. In reality, woodworking is really simple to learn. You'll most definitely want everything to be designed, and that's what you'll think about. Woodworking is the process of lifelong learning, but it is always one project at a time. So learning this way keeps you clever, but never overwhelms you with so much at a time.

It Is a Hazardous Activity

A major misconception about woodworking is the fact that everyone has fewer than ten fingers. Although there are few people like such in the business, tools are generally made for being safe. It's the users of the devices that aren't really secure, and because nobody wants to accept accountability anymore, they accuse the machine when they are injured. Woodworking machines include rotating wheels, revolving pieces, and shifting sections. When used wrongly, they will seriously damage you or yet disable you. However, the reality is you have complete authority over the situation. You can safely operate the tools for woodworking for the rest of the life if you spend some time learning the tool, learning about safety, and learning how to use it.

Wood Is Not a Good Material to Work with

Wood is a great material and has been used for thousands of years by humans. Wood is plentiful, varies in density, and can be a very powerful material for many projects. You will find smooth, strong, and very lightweight wood. Metalworkers criticize woodworking and they bring the obvious factor that the metal is substantially stronger than the wood. They're right, and that is a statement that is absolutely true. The reason modern woodworkers misunderstand it is that they think that metal is tougher, wood is weaker and that isn't the case. Most houses are made of wood as wood is frequently used as a building material. If it were a poor construction material, it might have become useless for the building of houses.

Woodworking Demands Physical Involvement

Of course, physical work would be required, even with the sharpest devices, but it's not as the misconception implies. Actually, this funny woodworking misconception comes from the woodworkers themselves. The misconception is that becoming a woodworker needs a lot of physical energy. It needs a lot of bodily effort to push hand planes, carve with sanding, chisels, etc.

If your hardened weapons, chisel, hand plane, etc., make your muscles sweat and fatigue when you're using them, then you must pause and sharpen your devices.

You Might Get Hurt by the Chemicals Used in the Woodworking Projects

Wood finishing is getting a bad image from those who don't even understand much about utilizing chemicals and wood finishes. Even If you do something stupid with chemicals, such as drinking them, they turn out to be extremely hazardous and most likely deadly. If you're cautious, however, and follow the manufacturer's safety recommendations, they may be extremely safe. The new woodworkers have a tendency to have little knowledge of handling chemicals. This can be addressed as it only needs limited knowledge of safety measures. Any of the finishes are intended to be controlled in some way, depending on what's inside the mix. Follow the manufacturer's instructions and you should have a pretty safe period. You should generally use a face mask, gloves, a respirator, and safety glasses. Work inside a greatly ventilated area and get someone to spot if you don't know how you're going to feel about a particular chemical.

You Cannot Start Woodworking Unless You Have a Big Dedicated Place

One of the worst is the misconception that you might need a large area to become a successful woodworker because this makes you think that it's an area that makes projects and not you. A determined woodworker may make a dining table within a reasonably average space if he concentrates on it, and a poor woodworker couldn't make the single cut into the best workshop in the world. As long as you have an inviting, comfortable, and creative woodworking space, then you've got a perfect shop. The rest are just the details, and this includes the size. It is who you decide what comes in from the shop, not size, not tools, not anything else but just you.

You Will Hurt Yourself by the Dust

The sawdust in the air can be dangerous when you are not protecting yourself. Again, dust is itself presented as the most detrimental element in woodworking, and people who make that statement still overlook that there are ample choices to keep themselves protected. When you don't do anything to defend yourself from the floating dust when something bad happens, you have no one to hold guilty other than yourself. With time, dust in the lungs may cause issues of health. The small particles are impossible to extract from the body, so they get trapped. This will contribute to breathing problems, asthma, and other debilitating diseases that will seriously shorten your life. Luckily, what you have to do is to invest in a proper machine to cover yourself from dust, so you will have a nice long workshop existence without the risk of something bad going as big as that. Simple devices aren't very costly, and they also filter the air that you breathe. Others are also costlier and look like biologically hazardous helmets. Those are further advanced filters that also offer face protection to protect against impacts.

The Woodworking Projects Are Time-Consuming

Some of the woodworking projects take a long time. However, this misconception falls separately real quickly as not all the projects are very involved. You can make pens, wooden rings, or more tiny things. In one day, you may really make a few of them. On the contrary, larger tasks may take days, otherwise weeks to accomplish. Wooden rings may be created by dozen in a single day, and there are a lot of finalized projects that are all done rapidly.

The Bottom Line

Your task is to see if some of those woodworking theories keep us back from getting started. If they don't, then now you should have the freedom to start without worrying. These are all complete myths, after all, and nothing that should ever prevent you from receiving into woodworking. So if you're still stuck and require some help, then do little extra research, please. You may find projects where you can get into woodworking without sacrificing anything too big or spending so much money. It's all related to you, again, and your wish to make wood projects. Due to a few myths, it is sad to see somebody does not begin with such a rewarding interest as woodworking. Woodworking is just so incredible. When they say that they won't start as one of the myths, you need to help others out. If any of these holds you back, then consider yourself liberated. You're going to do some research and you can overcome any of the myths.

1.12 Why should children be taught woodworking?

There is a great need for teaching woodworking to children from the beginning of their education. Most are astonished by the idea of the young children that are working with the real tools. However, in early childhood schooling, woodwork really equips the child with certain skills that become part of their personality when they grow up. As kids make different things from wood, they learn skills that consequently empower them to shape their world. It has almost vanished in the recent decades, but now it is making a return with concerted attention from all over the world. There is really something special about woodworking; it varies so much from other practices. The smell of wood and its feel, using the real tools and working with natural material, hammering and sawing sounds, minds and hands working altogether to convey the image and solve problems, using coordination and strength: all combined with captivating the interest of young children. It makes for a truly exceptional experience. Nonetheless, steps must be taken to ensure the safety of children. Woodwork is, in fact, a low-risk action as long as certain basic security measures are set in place and the appropriate tools are used. At the woodworking table, the behavior of children is outstanding—they are active and doing everything they love. It is often critical that children in a regulated environment face danger and difficulty in such a way that they acquire to make choices and assessments to defend themselves. That is an important characteristic of the development of children. Teachers who engage students in woodworking report observing extraordinary levels of children engagement on a regular basis. Children work on exciting projects with extensive focus and concentration accompanied by persistence and perseverance. They learn to embrace challenging tasks and thus equip themselves with the necessary complex problem-solving skills.

Woodworking Helps Children Develop Creative and Analytical Skills

Woodworking is a delightful medium for creative and expressive art. Mathematical calculations are developed, scientific knowledge is expanded, technological understandings are developed by working with the tools, and as they build, children become engineers. Woodwork is excellent for developing the critical and creative thinking skills of children as the children tinker and experiments with the possibilities of the wood and tools and go on expressing ideas and solving their work. However, woodwork isn't only about what kids do, It's all about changes that happen inside the kid. Woodwork has a significant influence on the self-esteem and self-confidence of children and it improves the sense of activity—that mindset of "can-do." Woodwork is a medium for the children to show their imagination and creativity. It's vital not to fix projects through which all kids create the same object. The key to children being truly interested in woodwork is the fact that they pursue their own desires to build their work and solve their own issues. When it is initiated, all examination becomes further meaningful and is ran by the children. Through this way of developing their critical and creative thinking skills, they'll lay the foundations for becoming future creative innovators. Initially, their task is often solely creative-tinkering with products and working out the different equipment possibilities. So they will show their creativity in a range of creative forms, producing works that they find interesting individually. They settle for more complex constructions, from literal works to more abstract and representational work.

Woodworking Helps Children Acquire and Develop Practical Skills

The woodworking process combines design and practical skills. Designs involve defining the task, drawing up an action plan, deciding on how to continue, and refining and responding appropriately as work develops. Older children might also desire to draw a few initial designs to help articulate the ideas.

Woodworking processes develop the building knowledge of children. They'll unavoidably join in woodwork and build in a range of unlike ways. They determine that flat-edged sections of wood are easier to attach than the angled pieces. So they learn how to create strong and robust joins or how to create their stand-up model. Kids become designers, artists, builders, architects, and sculptors as they build.

CHAPTER 2:

Evolution of Woodworking

Woodworking has been extensively used in art, philosophy, agriculture, leisure sporting events, and survival throughout history. Humans have been capable of hunting more successfully, build shelters, make boats and make things easier by learning woodworking skills. Wood was used to make bowls, spoons, and furniture and was also created as art. Woodworking actually contributed to society's progress. For the ancient Egyptians, Jews, Romans, Greeks, and all the other early cultures, woodworkers were a very significant part of the culture over 2000 years ago. Wooden furniture, like beds, benches, tables, stools, and chests, was portrayed in many paintings. Many fascinating facts relating to these antique woodworkers have been listed below.

- Coffins were also made from wood by the early Egyptians.
- Early Egyptians had invented the technique of veneering in the tomb of the Semerkhet, who had died more than 5000 years ago. With artifacts that have had the African ivory inlays and ebony veneer, many of the pharaohs were buried.
- Egyptians were first to 'finish' or varnish the woodwork, according to some historians, but nobody knows the composition of the 'finishes.'
- The Mortise and Tenon joints were used by ancient Egyptians for joining wood. These joints were strengthened by dowels, pegs, and leather.
- Around 1570–1069 B.C, Egyptians began to use animal glue.
- The traditional tools of the early Egyptian woodworker were axes, adzes, chisels, pull saws, and bow saws.
- The art of woodworking was also encouraged by early Chinese civilizations. Woodworking is thought to have mushroomed in the global community beginning around 720 B.C. at the time this happened. Chinese developed several advanced woodworking applications, including exact measurements utilized for creating bowls, tables, and other furniture parts.
- Woodworkers nowadays who perform prehistoric oriental woodworking methods are proud of their knowledge of fitted joints and their technique of not consuming electrical tools, glue, or nails to hold together different wood pieces. Japan is the place where this woodworking style mostly emerged.
- One explanation for Japan's success in outstanding woodworking has been that early in their history, they invented steel tools of high-carbon.
- Japanese woodworkers have created exquisitely-sculpted landscapes. Their success and the processes used in the process have spread through Southeast Asia.
- As soon as the carpenter wanted wood, with the assistance of other workers, he sawed the trees into the boards with the help of a big bronze saw.

From the tree trunks, he would cut skinny boards. However, trees in the area were not big or straight.

- The saw, adze, mallet, plummet and line, rule stick, chisel, plane, and squares were among the carpenter's tools that have been mentioned in ancient sources. They often used a bow drill, which they easily put in the motion through drawing bow attached back and forth, held in one hand by the handle.

- Bow-lathe has been a raw primitive instrument, but with it, a professional woodworker could make decorative spindles and bowls much like the woodturners of today. By pulling the strap of leather back and forth just like a bow, he turned the wood. This motion pushed lathe and permitted the making of cut in turning wood.

- Former woodworkers from the Near East constructed a great wood boat out of the timber that grew along the Levantine coast in the Anatolian plateau (Asian part of Turkey) (these are Mediterranean lands on the coast of present-day Syria, Turkey, and Lebanon). The said wood was prized that it was frequently requested as a tribute by invading armies.

- Archaeologists also discovered furniture made of wood veneered with ivory, bone, or bronze dating back to 800 B.C., the presumed residence of the legendary King Midas, at Gordion. Lathes and wedges, mallets, drills, compasses, chisels, plumb bobs, hammers, and other fundamental tools were used by Near East woodworkers.

- At the height of ancient Near East wood carving, the wooden window of private houses and early mosques still found today in Arabic cultures were constructed. For wall linings, ceilings, pulpits, and all sorts of fittings and furnishings, Muslim woodcarvers of Egypt, Persia, Syria, and Spain crafted and produced attractive paneling and other decorations. They were elaborate and minutely delicate in their woodwork.

With their expertise and inventiveness, woodworkers have been prized in the prehistoric world for their skills, setting the basis for today's woodworking. From ancient tools like chisels, lathes, saws, all the tools we use nowadays have been developed. The process of woodworking also came from the ancient craftsmen, and what they accomplished with 'primitive' tools is incredible.

It is evident from the above-mentioned facts that each culture in the world has utilized wood to build functional, also beautiful and artistic artifacts throughout ancient history, before our modern age. We see samples of ancient Greeks, Romans, Egyptians, and Chinese woodworking. Many more ancient cultures also practiced woodworking around the world, making use of many other styles and techniques. Primitive weapons used for hunting and defense have been utilized throughout the ages, as well as simple tools were used to build shelters. Archeologists have discovered digging sticks and wooden clubs at the Kalambo Falls in Kalambo River at the Zambia-Tanzania border. As the man developed the woodworking skills, so he turns out to be better able for killing animals for clear land, food for growing crops with his axis, and buildings, build boats, and furnishings. Thus, woodworking became an important process that led to civilizations' advancing. We will focus on some of the most famous cultures because of the large amount of content pertaining to woodworking history.

Egyptians and Woodworking

Many antique Egyptian drawings, from 2000 B.C. picture wooden furnishings like chairs, beds, stools, beds, tables, chests, etc. There is also physical evidence of the wooden things, as most were found to be well-kept in gravesites due to the dry climate of the country. Even some of the coffins (sarcophagi) found in graves were made from wood. The Ancient Egyptian woodworkers have been noted for the daily practice of the craft and for the creation of techniques that improved the art for centuries to come. For example, they invented the art of veneering, which is the practice of pasting together thin pieces of wood. Egyptians are considered to be the first to "finish" or varnish their woodwork, according to certain historians, but nobody knows the nature of such "finishes." The finishing is the process of applying some form of protective sealant to wood products for protection. Several of the tools were used by ancient Egyptian woodworkers including adzes, axes, chisels, bow drills, and pull saws. They also utilized mortise and Tenon joints for connecting pieces of the wood during the earliest pre-dynastic era. Those joints were strengthened by dowels, pegs, and cord lashings or leather. It was also found that during the New Kingdom period (1570 to 1069 B.C.) animal glue was used. Egyptologists discovered the oldest plywood piece in a coffin from the Third Dynasty. This was made up of 6 layers of 4 mms' thick wood which were held jointly by the wooden pegs. Egyptians used a range of wood to construct their furnishings and different objects. Wood originated in local sycamore trees, native acacias, and tamarisks. Nonetheless, when deforestation started in the Second Dynasty in Nile Valley, they started importing Aleppo pine, cedar, oak, and boxwood from different parts of the Middle East. They also obtained ebony from the Egyptian settlements and used this to create artifacts that went to tombs like wooden boxes.

The Ark of Noah and Advantages of Woodworking Skills

We find one of the first woodworkers of the Bible in the Book of Genesis—Noah. After God exposed His plan of destroying the corrupt human race by flooding the earth, He then gave Noah a 120-year project—to build a pitch-coated ark of cypress wood inside and outside.

God issued detailed orders and measurements for him and his three daughters. The ark was supposed to be 300 cubits long, 50 cubits wide, and 30 cubits high. So if we change cubits to feet based on the Hebrews' normal cubit of 17.5 inches, we get an ark minimum of 450 feet extended, 75 feet wide, and 45 feet high (about the size of the building of 4-story).

The ark's overwhelming scale staggers the mind, and for Noah and his daughters, it appears a daunting mission. However, the Scriptures do not say that without the aid of hired people Noah needed to create the ark. After all, for such a large vessel, the scale of timbers would probably have been further than the managing capabilities of four people. The ark has come to rest on Ararat's mountains after the flood. The Ararat Mountains are located in modern-day Turkey.

Woodworkers of Solomon's Time

While Noah and his woodworking team displayed excellent skills in the construction of the ark, during Solomon's time Hebrew Bible show other pictures of Israelite woodworkers. As it's written in Chapter 5 of 1 King, so Solomon needed to import the Phoenician artisans to build his temple from the coastal town of Tire. The Phoenicians were specialized in complex woodworking, like creating furniture and inlaying it with ivory carvings; however, as years went on, the woodworking abilities of the Israelite increased. In Isaiah 44 by 13, the prophet identifies the carpenter and his equipment, indicating that the Israelites were more skilled and specialized in carpentry throughout the reign of the kings. Carpenters were actually among the Israelites who were expelled to Babylon soon after Jerusalem was captured by the Babylonians in 597 B.C. The Lebanese cedar, which was imported by Lebanon, was considered as one of the most well-known building materials utilized by ancient woodworkers in the Biblical world due to the high quality, pleasing aroma, and resistance to both rot and insects. Many mosques, seagoing vessels, and palaces were constructed with wood, including the famous Temple of Solomon. The cedar was also used in the first century A.D. construction of the supposed "Jesus Boat." Two brothers had discovered a boat on the Sea of Galilee's northwest shore in 1986, after an incredible drought that had lowered water level. This was identical to the vessels Jesus used to enter and search the Sea of the Galilee, and his apostles. Nearly 27 ft. long and more than 7 ft. wide, types of the nails and the hull construction on the boat placed the origin of the boat between the 100 B.C. and 100 A.D.; this was the first nearly-finished boat on the Sea of the Galilee at that time.

China and Woodworking Techniques

The practice of woodworking was also encouraged by early Chinese cultures and civilizations. Woodworking in the country is believed to have mushroomed starting about 720 B.C. While it occurred, the Chinese created other advanced woodworking techniques, including detailed measurements that were used to produce bowls, tables, and other furniture parts. Lu Ban, a popular carpenter, has been recognized as one of the originators of woodworking in China during that time. It's believed that he brought to China the plane, the chalk line, and other tools. His wisdom was collected in the book "Manuscript of the Lu Ban" (Lu Ban Jing), about 1500 years after his death. This book described his job as a carpenter and included explanations of the measurements to create different items—such as tables, altars, and flower pots, it also offered detailed guidelines on Feng Shui (water and wind).

Contribution of Japanese to Woodworking

Today, woodworkers who learn ancient oriental woodworking technique takes pride in the knowledge of the designed joint and their determination not to use electrical tools, nails, or adhesive to tie together their parts. That style of woodworking originated primarily in Japan. One reason that could be ascribed to Japan's success in very brilliant woodworking was that early in their history they had developed the steel tools of high carbon. The usage of high-quality blades and lathe engineering made leading prehistoric Japanese woodworkers in the crafting of round and curved objects. In Japan, cooperage (making barrels) and bentwood works (the wood falsely shaped for use in furniture making) were popular for daily household items.

Japanese woodworkers have also produced exquisitely sculpted sceneries. The popularity and techniques utilized in this process have spread throughout Southeast Asia.

Woodworking in Christ's Era

Carpenters in Jesus' day were frequently called upon to build or repair threshing sleds or plows or cut roofing beams, or form yokes for the new oxen team. They fulfilled demands for the new doors and door frame, or chest for safety, and rendered a number of fixes. Occasionally, they helped build bigger building projects like building a wooden balcony or manufacturing stairs or doors for a new synagogue. On some occasions, a master carpenter will be questioned to create a sacred object like a Torah cabinet to store scrolls of scripture. Hebrew carpenters utilized different species of wood depending on the job's requirement. They included oak, cypress, ash, olive, and sycamore. They may also have to import costly cedar from Lebanon or utilize stock of the vines for tiny projects if it was a special project. When the carpenter wanted wood, with the help of other workers, he saw trees in boards, using a huge bronze saw. He sliced thin boards off the trunks of a tree. However, trees in the region weren't big or straight. The saw, adze, mallet, plummet and chisel, line, plane, rule stick, and squares were among the carpenter's tools mentioned in ancient sources. They also used a bow drill, held by a handle in one hand, which they quickly set in motion by drawing back and forth on the attached bow. Bow-lathes were a simple primitive instrument, but a professional woodworker was able to create elegant spindles and bowls along with this, much like the woodturners of today. He twisted the wood, pulling back and forth like a bow with a leather cord. This motion shifted the lathe and made it possible to make the cut in the woods. With the tools in hand, Biblical-era carpenters had the ability to create mitered, intricately dovetailed, and dowelled joints. They frequently created impressive wooden products combining considerable skill with patience.

Woodworking in the Middle East

The woodworking in the Middle East, as shown in the explanations of those objects, dates back several decades, spreading to Biblical times. The Book of Exodus, for example, chronicles the construction of the holy wooden objects for the ancient Hebrew Tabernacles.

The ancient Near East woodworkers constructed great timber wooden boats that grew up on the Anatolian plateau (Asian part of Turkey) alongside the Levantine coast (coastal Mediterranean lands of present-day Syria, Lebanon, and Turkey). The wood was very prized, that it was always requested as a ransom by foreign armies. Wedges, chisels, mallets, hammers, axes, compasses, plumb bobs, and other simple devices were used by woodworkers in the Near East. Syria, Persia, Egypt, and Spain's Muslim woodcarvers crafted and produced attractive paneling and other accessories for floors, wall linings, pulpits, and fittings, and furniture of all sorts. The woodwork was elaborate and exquisitely delicate.

Romans and Professional Woodworking

Roman Empire had the share of professional woodworkers as well. Equipped with adzes, lathes, logs, boats, saws, and drills, like the bow weapon, they constructed waterworks and aqueducts using the wooden scaffolding, designed magnificent barges and warships and installed strong and deadly battering rams and catapults to assault enemy towns. They also crafted the furniture, including chairs and tables that represented animal arms in a stylistic way or were imprinted to represent the mythological creatures. Roman woodworkers made their wooden crafts from a variety of trees. Species of wood included beech, ilex, pine, elm, oak, and ash.

How Did Woodworking Survive in the Middle Ages?

Because in the Middle Ages wood was the most public building material, carpenters prospered. Also, they were considered among the most skilled artisans. Carpenters had to do the apprenticeships with existing carpenters. Their devices were far better than whatever we are using now, but they needed to learn how to utilize them and practice math and woodwork. To build wagons, homes, and furniture for citizens of that age—including kings and lords—this information was important. Each of the houses still used timber. Many houses were made nearly completely out of timber, from the frame for the walls and roofs to the siding and shingles. But buildings made of stone required substantial wooden construction. Although most of the Middle Age wooden buildings have long since disappeared, we still have modern illustrations of the buildings and other wood structures either finished or under construction.

2.1 Woodworking Advantages

Listed below are some of the key benefits of woodworking:

- It is about using renewable, biodegradable, and non-toxic resource—wood—to make you, your friends, and your family use environmentally friendly and healthy items
- Crafted pieces are lovely and special, and they make perfect gifts
- The woodworking skills allow you to carry out home repairs
- Woodworking is good for you—it's meditative, therapeutic, hobby or career-friendly
- It's a good exercise, and you can save money
- It is just perfect for you, especially if you're really keen (and good) on starting a small business and helping to steer some money away from the omnipresent flat-pack giants
- Environmental and fitness advantages are stronger if you use hand tools – lower energy usage and no resources required, only muscle strength
- The environmental advantages become much better if such hand tools become second-hand; often, older tools are constructed of very high-quality material, surpassed today by the machinery of the same size
- Wood is very durable, as wooden objects, if well-made, can last several lifetimes, and solid wooden furniture is very fixable. There is immense joy in creating products that can be passed down across generations, but even though they come to the end of their lives, they can be recycled or used as firewood instead of the landfill
- It can stimulate local timber demand, and thus tree planting

2.2 Primitive Woodworking Tools Still in Use

Primitive is a term describing something that is ancient or outdated. When anyone claims it's very primitive, they generally mean that nowadays, it's not the same as it used to be. Typically, defining anything primitive means the device won't stand up well in contradiction of the device's current version. Over time, circumstances change and improve. Soon enough, original versions of something becomes unrecognizable with the latest version. With that being said, certain aspects of the initial design remain pretty much the same. Here are few primitive tools we're all using nowadays.

Bow and Arrow

A device that has been used for many years is the bow and arrow. Many scholars claim that in Africa, the instrument originated about 64,000 years before. They took the arrows and bows with them as people migrated across the world. The arrow and bow gradually became a weapon that had multiple uses. The instrument was originally used for hunting for food. Yet, it quickly became a weapon against mankind when populations and cultures launched wars. We're all using the arrow and bow today. It is used as a recreational shooting weapon in western parts of the world or during sporting (archery) competitions. A tool used to hunt and provide food is now used in other parts of the world.

The Axe

One of the oldest weapons that are still utilized today is the hand axe. Most suggest that during the Stone Age, it originated about 1900000 years ago and continued to evolve and change over the ages. It is believed that the first-hand axe was made of nothing other than refined stones of pear-shape. This lacked a shaft as well. It built a shaft for the swinging over the years. For hunting, cutting, slicing, and even fighting, the hand axe was and is used as a weapon. Today, with all kinds of occupations and activities, we still use the axe and its many variants.

Hammer

Hammer has a somewhat close history to hand axe. Hammer is a tool that was soon used for building and civilized development (although it may have been used in fighting and hunting). Once upon a time, it was nothing more than blunted stone. With civilization, the hammer developed into molded iron shaft pieces that were utilized to strike nails into the wood and smash and wedge stuff together. Many other hammers exist today. On several job sites today, fiberglass shaft with steel heads and nail removal hooks are common. For a long time, the hammer was around and will most probably be around forever.

Saw

The origin of saws initiated from unusual materials like seashells and flint. Metal-workers continued to produce saws from iron and copper as technology progressed. For cutting different materials, new saws were sharper, better, and more powerful. While saws weren't (reliably) referred to as a weapon, there are incidents where saws were used as tools of torture and for executions. Though, we are past those days. Nowadays, saws are used mostly for manufacturing.

Knives

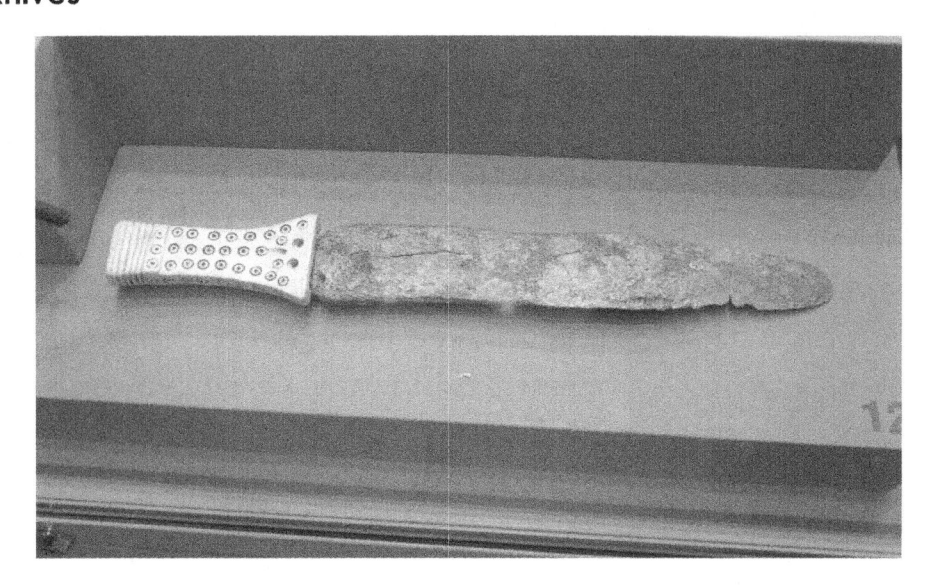

Knives are one of the primitive most versatile tools we still use today. Knives have numerous tasks that they can do, whether they discover the use in slicing fruit, self-defense, surgical purposes, or hunting. The origin of the knife is thought to have been initiated from the axe by many. The knife remained pretty much as its original version, like the axe. For knives, different materials, like steel, iron, and even ceramic composites, are now used. The first knives were made sometimes from sharp seashells, stones, and animal bone. Today, on a regular basis, much of the world still use knives. The knife was one of the most basic tools in the world and one of the greatest and most commonly used tools in the world.

2.3 Essential Information

Axes and adzes were amongst the first tools to be made. Woodworkers used axes to fell the trees and adzes to dress the timber, the blade of which was turned 90 degrees. In Egypt, the handsaw had been used as long ago as 1500 B.C. This had broad blades, few up to twenty inches, curved handles in wood, and irregular teeth in metal. They were to pull and not push because blades were of copper, soft metal. Since the carpenter couldn't bear on cutting motion, sawing wood would have been a boring, sluggish operation. The Romans got the handsaw improved in two ways. For the blades, they used the iron, making it stiffer, and they set saw's teeth to project the alternately left and right. This allowed the saw to cut somewhat wider than the blade, making for a smoother motion. Also, the Romans invented a frame saw and stiffened the back of the saw, with a blade reinforced at the top to provide straight-through cutting. Using a thin blade carried in a wooden frame, the frame saw is kept stretched by tightening thread. The Frame Principle saw modern hacksaw live on. Roman builders had used tools developed by the ancient Egyptians, try square (also known as carpenter's square), plumb line, and chalk line. Instead of nails, Egyptian woodworkers used wooden pegs also and made holes with bow drills that they had moved back and forth. Because bow drill seems to be useless for hard digging and wastes time and energy, a stronger method came up for the Romans: auger. Auger has a short cross-handle of wooden attached to the steel shaft with spoon-shaped bits at its tip. It allowed the woodworker to exert high rotational force and heavy pressure downward. Middle-aged woodworkers built breast augers to dig large holes in the timbers of vessels. It is surmounted by broadsheet, on which carpenter laid all his body weight.

By inventing cast-iron nails, the Romans built on the wooden pegs of the Egyptians. They made another dual-use tool as well: a claw hammer. On top of this, the Romans created the law, smooth plane, and many other plane forms. One historian called the wood plane "the most significant advance in the woodworking tool history." The chisels are perhaps primitive devices. Carpenters from the Bronze Age used them as integrals. Good forests have blanketed most parts of the world throughout human history. They provided a valuable and abundant resource for civilization: wood. The wood was easier to be working with and an easy to shape material, so it was used in many different ways by the artisans. They developed wood arms and siege equipment. They built temples, houses, boats, plows, furniture, and even coffins that used local wood, or imported aromatic, fine woods from the distant lands for special needs. They also sculpted wooden statues and more decorative pieces. Following the erection of stone structures, woodworkers used wood scaffolding to aid in the construction. As the civilizations advanced, new tools for cutting and shaping wood were invented, or existing ones were improved. Most woodworkers' hand tools used nowadays have changed little since ancient times.

CHAPTER 3:

Learn to Use Woodworking Tools Every Woodworker Needs

Every skill has its tools, and there is no exception with woodworking. Any craftsman knows that in producing a quality end product in a timely manner, the appropriate tool for the project is critical. You can find carpenter tools, woodworking power tools, woodshop tools, and the best woodworking tools in the list of tools listed below. Moreover, this chapter will help beginners who feel overwhelmed when trying to understand which hand tools they need first. Here's a summary of the top woodworking tools that every woodworker, as well as carpenter, should think about owning.

3.1 Essential Woodworking Hand Tools

Woodworking hand tools get their hardness from your muscles. They are tools of power but not electrical power. A complete list of hand tools that every woodworker, cabinet maker, or carpenter should think about having in his woodshop is given below.

The Claw Hammer

Let's start with perhaps the most basic tool, the claw hammer, in every household. The claw should be well counterbalanced by the finished head on one side of the head, which should be rounded somewhat. The waffle-head is the other type of head. Most often used in construction, when you drive the nail, it leaves a distinctive waffle mark on the wood. This is not the right nail for woodworking, of course. In your hand, a poorly balanced claw hammer would twist, making this problematic to properly drive the nails. You usually grip the claw hammer at the back to grip with your hand, allowing the weight of the head to do the maximum work. So all you have to do is point the driving surface to the right nail, avoiding the ones on hand. The size of the most demanding claw hammer is 20 oz. It is heavy enough to drive nails easily, but when pulling nails, it is easily manipulated. While wooden handles are quaint, if you have to be pulling a lot of the nails, they may not stand up to the strain. There are stronger hammers with steel handles or even fiberglass. However, these will not absorb vibrations from the driving nails as a hickory handle would. For control and comfort, you'll also require to ensure fiberglass and metal handles also have a rubberized grip. The wooden handled hammer would also be good for reducing the stress on the hand and wrist if you're going to drive a lot of nails.

The Tape Measure

The precise tape measure is the next significant hand tool for the woodworker. Get a retractable one that has a length of no less than 25 feet. Any longer, and you start having trouble getting it to roll. Because measurements on the large-scale plans could be quite vulnerable to even the smallest variations in measurement, you will want to ensure that the "hook" or tab at the tape's end is confidently attached, with no give. You will have as many as one by 8" variations in measurements when they get loose. In the long run, this could add up some serious accuracy issues.

The Utility Knife

Another asset for a woodworker is a fine utility knife. There are several different kinds. However, the most common is the type that utilizes disposable blades. For safety, the blade retracts into the grip. In addition to many other applications, the woodworker will be using utility knives while cleaning out the mortise joints and/or scribing wood.

The Moisture Meter

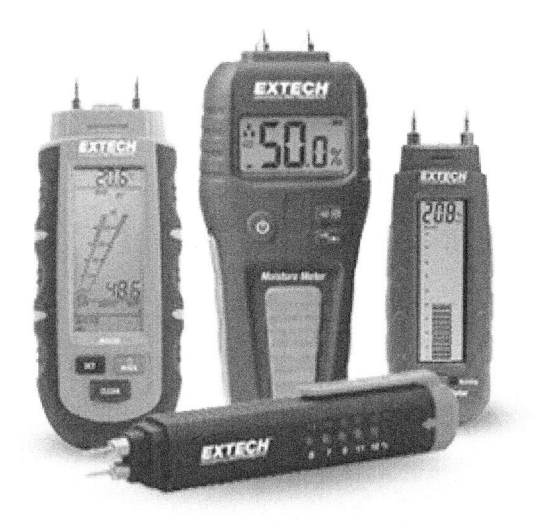

For the long-term success of every woodworking project, you put together, a quality wood moisture meter is important. According to the planned end product destination, lumber mills aim to dry their batches of lumber. That is if the wood is cut in the wet Northeast but is to be transported to the arid Southwest, more of the wood kept in the Northeast would be dry for woodworkers to use. From wood flooring to kitchen cabinets to fine furniture, the success of your woodworking project depends on the right moisture content levels of the woods that you use for your region of the country. There are moisture meters whose pins can penetrate the surface of the wood. This can leave small holes that mar the surface and need to be filled. Some are pin-less. They have sensing plates under them that scan the wood. Not all pin-less moisture meters, though, are the same. Look for one that uses equipment that is not compromised by wood surface moisture. Your best moisture meter should have settings that account for multiple wood species. Oak, for example, is a hardwood, but ebony is a much harder wood in density. You will need to know the moisture content levels of both species if you are planning an inlay job with both types of wood so that your inlay glue joints will remain intact. There are various unique gravities of these different wood types that must be used or programmed into the moisture meter. Therefore, before manufacturing a finished product, you must measure the wood species you are using in your woodworking project to ensure that they are at the correct moisture content.

The Level

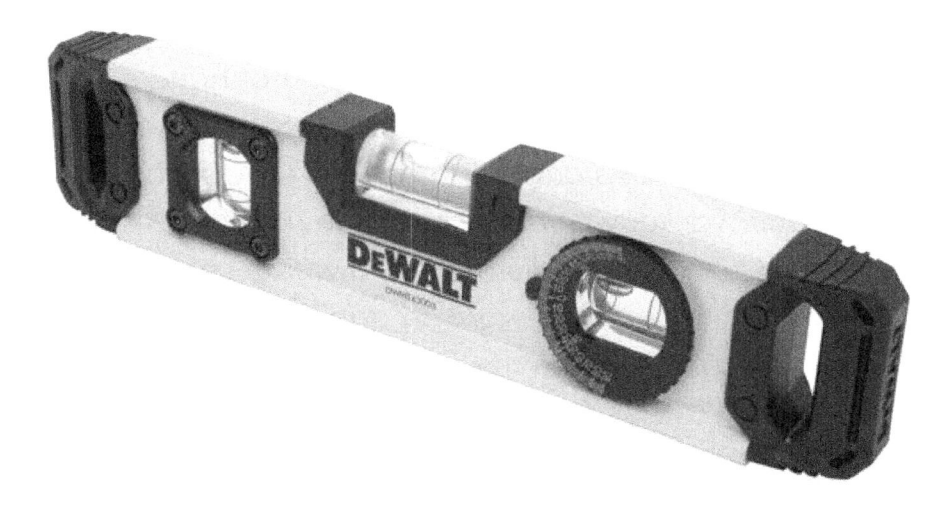

A couple of levels are needed by every woodworker. You probably won't need one of the six-foot levels used in the construction, but for most of the woodworking projects you'll do, a level of 48" is good enough. Usually, you will also require an 8-inch level, usually called torpedo level too. You'll be checking the plum and level of construction. Level refers to horizontal, and plumb is vertical. Most levels are created of either brass-edged metal or wood. There's going to be bubble reading for the level. There will also be one for the plumb. When the bubble is precisely between lines, you have level or the plumb surface. You can also get string and laser levels, but these will be used by the woodworker most often.

The Screwdriver

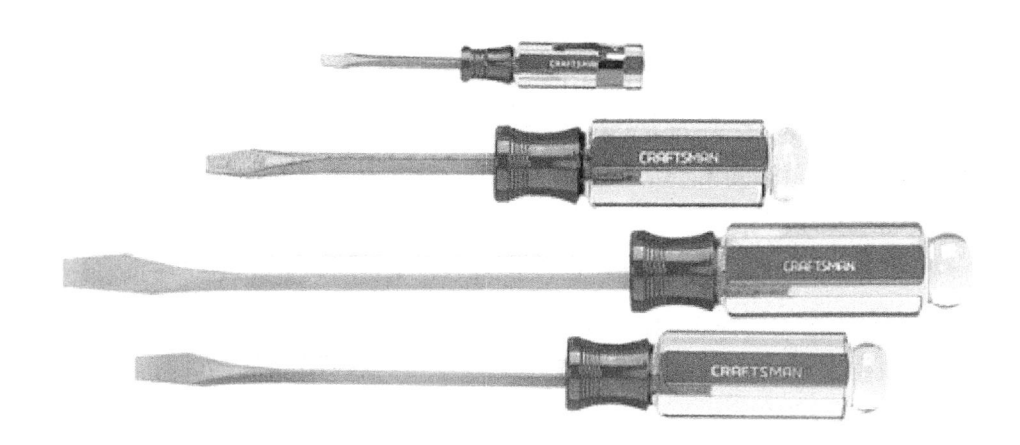

Another must-have in the woodworker's collection of hand tools are screwdrivers. You're not only going to need Phillips and slot or flathead screwdrivers, but you're still going to need star drivers and Torx drivers. You'll need a long, very heavy-duty screwdriver with a square blade. This creates a lot of torque for you. You need a small and medium slot screwdriver as well. You will require a screwdriver with a thin shank to work on cabinets or tight areas in woodworking so that you can handle screws that are inside deep holes. Through a cabinet screwdriver, this is accomplished. Get a few medium Phillips head screwdrivers for those tight spots and a stubby one, too. You may like a ratchet screwdriver as well. If the quality material of your slot screwdrivers is really high, you will be able to grind them flat while they get worn. Beware, however, that too much heat will modify the metal's temper, weakening it so that screws won't drive or draw. Given below are some techniques to help you use them in the most productive way:

- Choose the correct blade dimension for the screw.
- Fit the driver into the screw for stubborn screws, apply as much downward pressure as you can on the screwdriver, and hit the end with a hammer. It also assists with stripped-out screws.
- Before you drive screws into hardwood, apply beeswax on the threads of the screws. Use soap if you have no beeswax. This helps the screws to drive more effectively.
- With a shorter shank, you will get more driving ability.
- In order to get more torque, use a crescent wrench on the blade. A screwdriver may be magnetized by certain persons by holding it up and striking it with a metal bar. This realigns the molecules, which makes them magnetic. You can even damage your screwdrivers this way, so be careful. Bottom of Form
- Top of Form
- Bottom of Form

A Wooden Workbench

Wooden workbench has always been the center of the workshop of a traditional woodworker. You can escape with nearly anything that allows you to secure the wood in the place for planning and sawing if you are really on a tight budget and use the clamps for securing your workpiece.

You can either build a workbench of wood or buy one if you feel the construction of a workbench is too complex for yourself right now.

The Nail Set

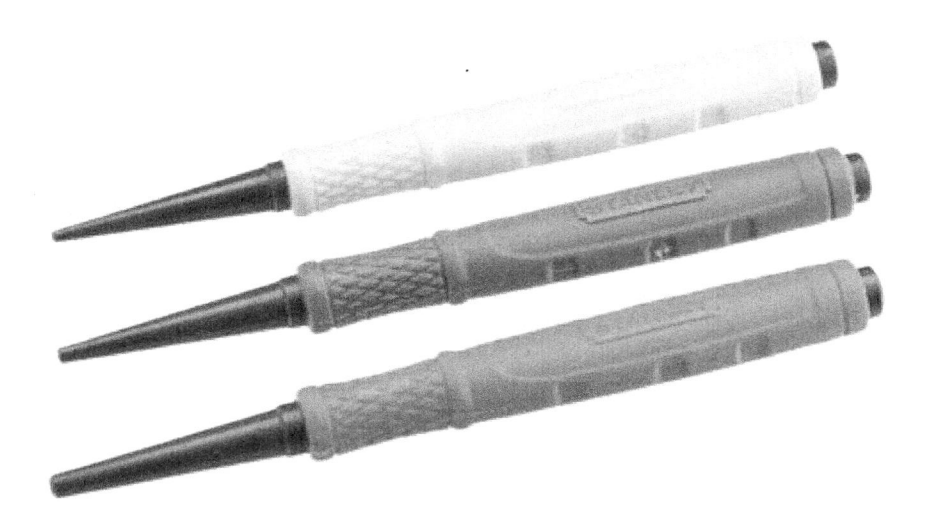

A nail set is the next hand tool that any woodworker should have. In truth, You can have many sizes. They look like awls and you use them to help you drive nail heads into the wood. This helps you to fill and prepare for staining or painting the holes. To grip the nail tighter to prevent it from slipping off and marring the wood, the nail setter will generally either have a convex or concave surface.

The Sliding Bevel

A sliding bevel, or T-Bevel, would be a handy instrument if you would have to measure a lot of angles. This is customizable and you could always lock it at the angle you select to mark, allowing several angles to be labeled and thus making it even more time-savvy.

The Sliding Bevel Square

For scribing angles on the workpiece, a moving bevel square (or "bevel gauge") is required. When fixed, a successful sliding bevel square will be able to replicate the angle, again and again, just like when you put down dovetails on the face of the board.

Not all the sliding bevel square is great to hold the angle, so ensure you've read more before you buy a bevel gauge.

A Jack Plane

A Jack Hand plane is a bench plane of middle size. There are planes that are so commonly used that they normally sit on the workbench. When you are on a budget, you can temporarily use Jack Plane instead of additional planes carrying out specialized functions:

Rough removal of stock (if you purchase second blade/iron and shape it in curved "camber")

To help joint edges of the board (as long as the board does not exceed 3x length of the Jack Plane)

For Smoothing of Surfaces

Eventually, you're going to want to buy a devoted jointer plane and smoothing plane. However, a Jack Plane would let you start working! A sharp and new low angled Jack Plane will be perfect for beginners and professionals who aren't up to rehab a hand plane.

A Block Plane

The Block planes, in a woodworker's workshop, is one of the most commonly employed tools. Some typical woodworkers in the aprons still hold them! You may use these tiny planes to trim the joints, position chamfers on the board sides, trim the end grains, etc. Finding a block plane of low angle is recommended because low angle makes it easier to cut problematic grain.

Get 2 Panel Saws: Rip and Cross Cut

Handsaws (frequently called the "panel saws") are large, skinny saws with sturdy wooden handles. They're used to scale the lumber. A panel saw is theoretically a smaller hand saw that fits into the panel of the tool chest. Panel saw comes in two tooth shapes. You are going to need both:

Rip

It cuts along grain like a chisel.

CrossCut

It cuts across the grain like a knife.

Panel saws are affordable. However, you must know what you are looking for exactly. Moreover, you should be keen to spend little time learning how to sharpen the hand saws.

Get 1–3 Back Saws

Unlike the panel saws, when making the wooden joints (such as dovetail joints), "back saws" are used for fine precision work. Thin metal plates of the saw are rendered rigid with brass or steel "backs," which extend around the top of saw plates.

If you're on a small budget, you might get away with a dovetail saw for the time being. But if you've meant, so then you should buy three back-saws:

Get a Miter Box and Miter Saw

A good miter saw and miter box (very big backsaw) allows you for cutting wood to very précised lengths, with precise angles. It will particularly save a lot of time trying to make the ends of your board square. Long miter saws typically glide back and forth through the rigid frame. The angles of the frame can be transformed to allow you for cutting perfect miter joint (joints used for image frames) and lots of other joints.

Pick up Coping Saw

A pick-up coping saw is used regularly in the board for uneven cutting shapes, but in particular to remove waste from dovetail joints (one of the most common joints of wood). A pick-up coping saw along with a pack of reasonable replacement blades will work finely.

A Bench Chisel Set

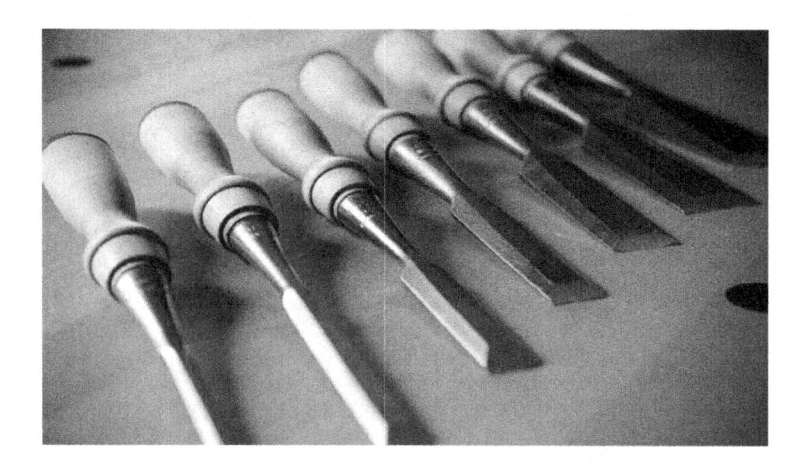

Chisels are used in the workshop more than some other tool. A high-quality collection of bench chisels, bevel edge (vintage or new) can last for several years and can be utilized on almost every project. A decent set of 7 or 5 bench chisels (these don't have to be matching) will immediately get going. Eventually, you'll attach those specialist chisels down the line (such as fishtail chisels, paring chisels, etc.); however, bench chisels should fit with just about anything.

The Chisel

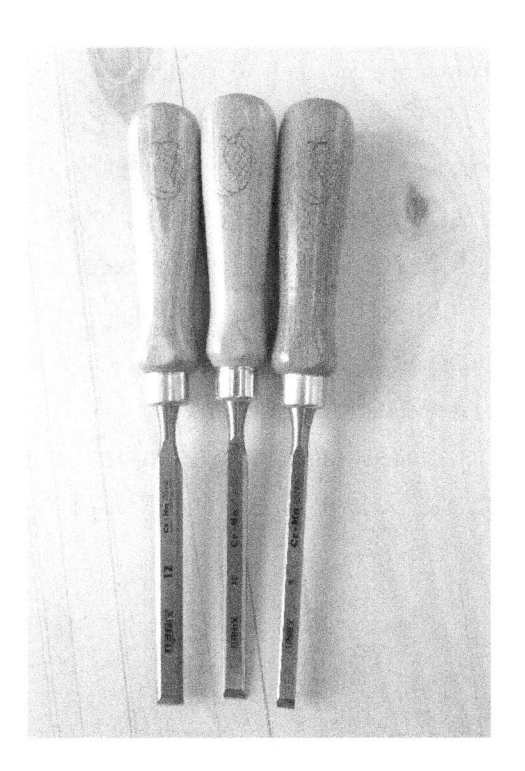

Any workbench should have a variety of chisels. Chisels aren't for woodcarvers alone. For cleaning out the joints and saw cuts, any woodworker would require chisels. Look for chisels made of great carbon alloy steel or chromium-vanadium alloy steel. The hardwood handles, particularly if they've metal caps above them, are best. This will prevent the end of the handle as you hammer on it from being malformed. The best sizes for you will be in 1/4" increments from 1x4" to a minimum of 1.5". The smallest chisels for the mortise work are the greatest. The 3/4" and 1" are perfect for the door hinges and for chipping out, the 1 1/2" works well. With the strike of a hammer, you can also get a corner chisel that cuts notch out of the wood. On two sides and on the cutting edge, most chisels are beveled, but specialist chisels might just be slanting at the cutting edge. The bevel would be on one side at twenty to 25 degrees down the length of the blade and flat on the backside. The blade is going to be between 4" and 7" long. Ensure you have chisels that fit your hand. You would not be able to keep the chisel steady while you operate if the grip is too small. When working, make sure of using a mallet or a wooden hammer so that you don't destroy the head of your chisel. Then Keep track of the edge cap. Also, keep it sharp, and once you've used them, oil metal now and then, and they must be fine for years. Even If you don't have the caps on edge, get a roll to hold them in. It will prevent them from bouncing around and getting broken in your toolbox drawers. Both hands are used while you work with the chisels. This helps the chisel to have strength and leverage as this pares the wood away. Butt-ends of the chisel can be broken by a claw hammer, finally splitting this if you mistreat it too much. You might need to utilize stones instead of the grinder when sharpening your chisel. To hone the blades properly, you require a collection of stones of progressively fine grit. The coarser grade is good to start with and the finest grade for finishes. For better results, you can need to dampen the stone with the oil. Moreover, you should always hone blades far away from the body.

Get a 6-inch Combination Square

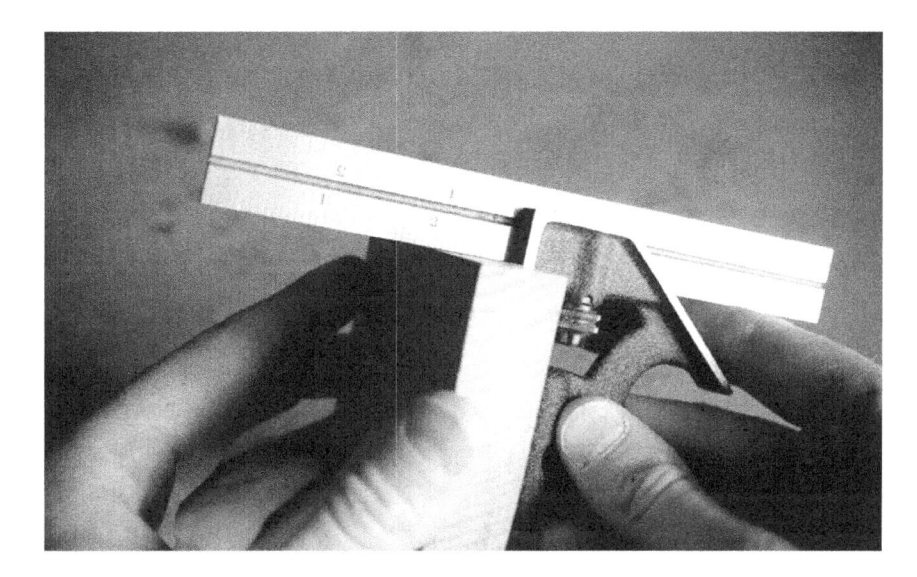

A very nice and precise 6-inch combination of the square can be used in the workshop for many activities like testing the squareness of frames. Square is also used to scribe dovetail joints, measure mortise depth, and much, much more.

Be vigilant when buying mix squares "at a reasonable price." Many are frequently machined incorrectly or "out of the square."

The Layout Square

A layout square, or combination square, is available in sizes 6" and 12". The 6" model is used by most woodworkers, mainly because it is easiest to carry around. Most of the stock you're going to use will also be no longer than 6 " wide, so 12 " is overkill. A triangle that you can use to mark square cuts on the stock is the layout square. You line up the layout square with the board's edge once you measure the length of the cut. A straight, square cut across the end grain will give you the short side. The layout square can also be used to measure angles. When you try to measure for a bevel on a table saw or mark a cut for a miter saw, this helps you. To determine an existing angle, you can also use your layout square. Only make sure that you purchase one made of metal. Not only are the plastic ones fragile, but they can even warp, making them pretty worthless.

3.2 Make a Try Square

For precision fitting of joints, try squares are used for squaring up your workpieces. If you are not yet confident enough of constructing your specific try square, you should buy a try square of good metal (between 12 and 9 inches somewhere). It will be used to scribe square lines about your board's faces and edges, such as a line for somewhere for cutting with the saw.

In fact, most squares aren't perfect 90 degrees or "square." However, you could use the file to convert it into a square.

3.3 Get a Pair of Dividers (Compass)

A compass (or dividers) is used on a piece of work to take and repeat a measurement over and over again. When doing fine joinery work, traditional woodworkers rarely take the measurements with a tape measure but instead take measurements with the dividers. Subsequently, they transfer that measurement to other pieces of work. This helps to get rid of inaccuracy. Also, dividers are used for arc scripting and much more. You will have a minimum of one "pair" of the dividers (1 compass), anywhere between a scale of 6-inch and 9-inch. It's also helpful to have a tiny pair of dividers (like three inches), so you can stock more than one measurement at one time.

3.4 Make a Marking Gauge

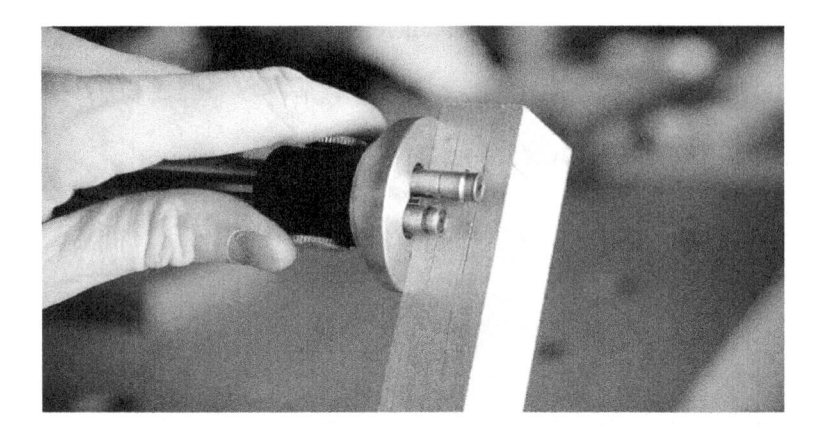

Like the dividers, marking the gauges can be used to transfer measurement and to repeat it all over again. A locking device prevents the gauge from slipping and losing the data. You cannot effectively construct furniture without having at minimum one decent, durable labeling scale. Having mortise gauges (with the two pins or cutters) is too convenient. However, you can certainly get through laying out the mortises with only one marking gauge. However, beware of cheaply-manufactured marking gauges. They're going to be useless and will result in wastage of money.

Pick a Folding Rule

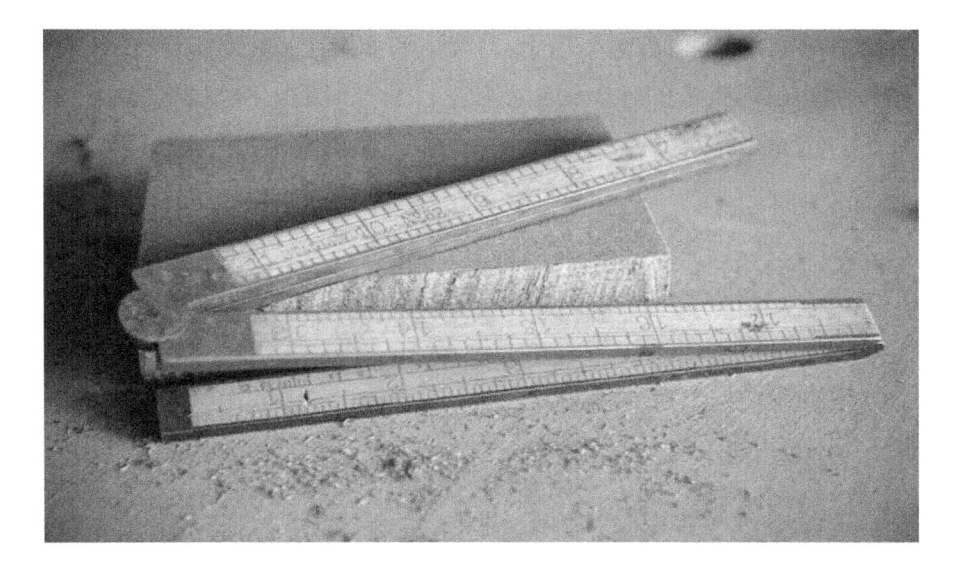

They are precursors of tape measure that allows measures to be made while cutting boards, etc. If you're on a tight budget, you may use a tiny tape measure for the same work, typically for the rough measurement. A good 24-inch antique wooden rule is so convenient to have since it slides into your apron or pocket and gives quick measurements. They're very cheap, but you should know what you're looking for.

Get Sharpening Supplies

One of the most important features of the proper old-style woodworking with the hand-held tool is having a very sharp tool. Most beginners think they don't perform well at woodworking. However, they usually only use dull (or inappropriately sharpened) hand tools. Purchasing quality sharpening materials for sharpening and honing the hand irons plane, chisels, and handsaws are strongly recommended, especially for beginners.

Make a Wooden Joiner's Mallet

For conventional woodworking, a strong wood mallet is important. The lighter carver's mallets won't be heavy-duty enough for maximum tasks, particularly chopping on a mortise chisel. The wooden mallet is often used to hit chisels while you are cutting joints (such as chopping mortises or dovetail joints). You must never try to hit the chisel with a metal hammer. Purchase or build a mallet made of just hardwood (example: maple, beechwood, oak, etc.) that will feel finely balanced in hand and give enough weight for chopping with chisels.

3.5 Get a Rabbet Plane

Rabbets are one of the most usual joints in the making of furniture, so a hand plane that cuts rabbet must be at the top of the tool list to buy. Without a hand plane, rabbets could be cut but with greater difficulty. Many hand planes, including the wooden rabbet planes, shoulder planes, metal planes rabbet, and planes of moving fillister, can cut rabbets. A wood or metal moving fillister plane (in the above picture) is most useful because it allows you to cut the rabbets across the grain and with the grain. It also allows you to cut panels easily (as grasped above). Movable fences really help with achieving precision.

Get a Couple of Woodworking Clamps

Woodworking clamp holds freshly glued joints altogether till glue hardens. It's suggested to purchase a minimum of one quality "hand screwed clamp" (around 10 or 20 inches) and a few bar-form or parallel clamps. However, before purchasing the clamps, construct the first project and put it together without the glue. And then witness how many of the clamps you'd think you'll be needing to put sufficient pressure into all right spots. So then ensue to buy that numbers of the clamps. Then repeat the process on the next project and buy additional clamps if required. It is better than to run out and buy huge collections of woodworking clamps. To see my purchasing guide for the different types of clamp, uses, and my favorite brands.

The Jig

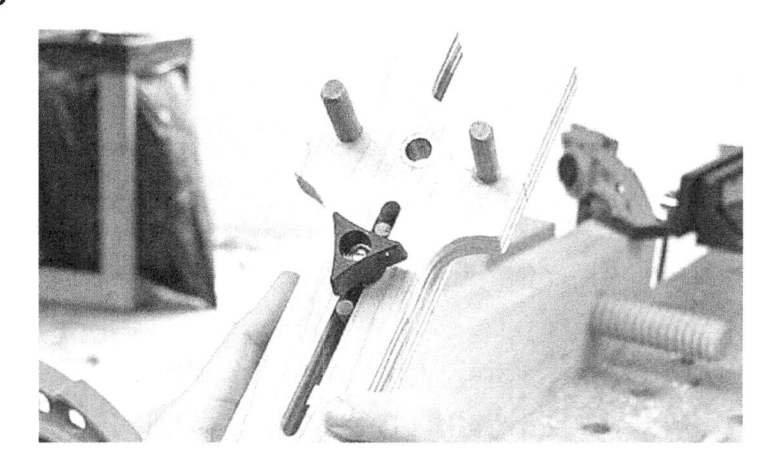

If you have jigs, you do not have to measure every single cut and joint. Some woodworkers build their own jigs. In order to guide the piece through the saw, you usually use a jig with a power tool. To cut a perfect circle, you can make a jig that you can use. You would need to make furniture with legs that are tapered. Without the trouble of re-marking the angles on each leg, a jig will do this. A dovetail jig does exactly that. As you make dovetail joints, it guides your wood.

The Hand Saw

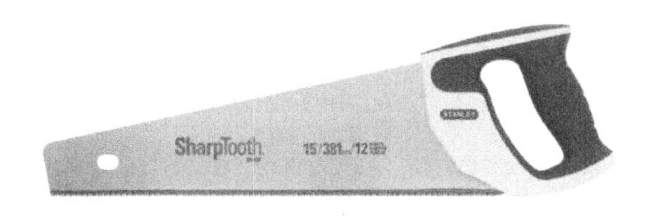

You should not overlook a high-quality hand saw. In fact, one of the most precious enhancements to your woodworking shop might be a select collection of hand saws. You don't have to use a power saw at all—you don't want to, really. You ought to be able to feel the reaction of the wood under the saw blade and the response of the saw blade to the wood. You will need a dovetail saw, and a hand miter saw as well, in addition to a coping and Tenon saw. In reality, for many woodworkers, the backbone of their craft is a fine set of Japanese saws. Start with a fretsaw for woodworkers for general use; it's like a coping saw for wood. For places in which a chisel simply won't work, you need a mini saw, too. Then, along with a miter box that you can use with the Tenon saw, a proper Tenon saw can follow. Other saws will come as the need arises, with their range of cutting surfaces and angles.

The Feather Board

Feather boards are necessary for obtaining smooth, quality cuts. To move the material past the cutting edge, you'll need a feather board for all sorts of saws, as well as other cutting surfaces. You can make feather boards of your own or buy them instead. It is better for most woodworkers to only make them suit their own needs.

The Metal Detector

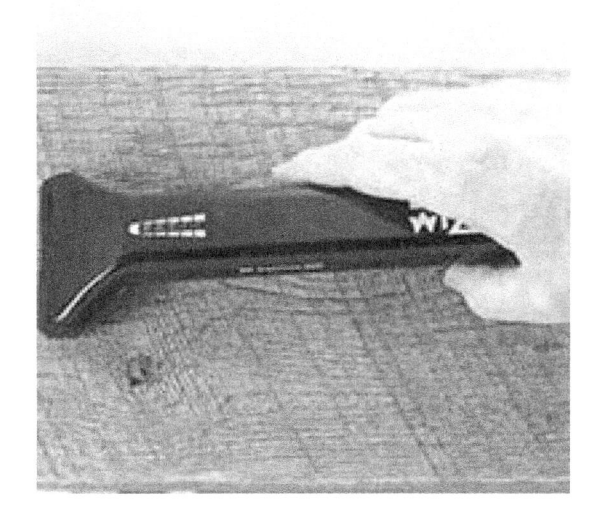

No, with your metal detector, you are not searching for buried treasure. You are looking for something that could damage your treasures, your woodworking tools. Keeping metal out of your cutting surfaces is of critical significance; otherwise, you can destroy your blades, bits, and knives. A swift search with a metal detector will also let you know if your stock is still carrying a piece of screw or nail. Anyway, you'll find out. It's just good to find out before you damage your tools.

The Tool Storage System

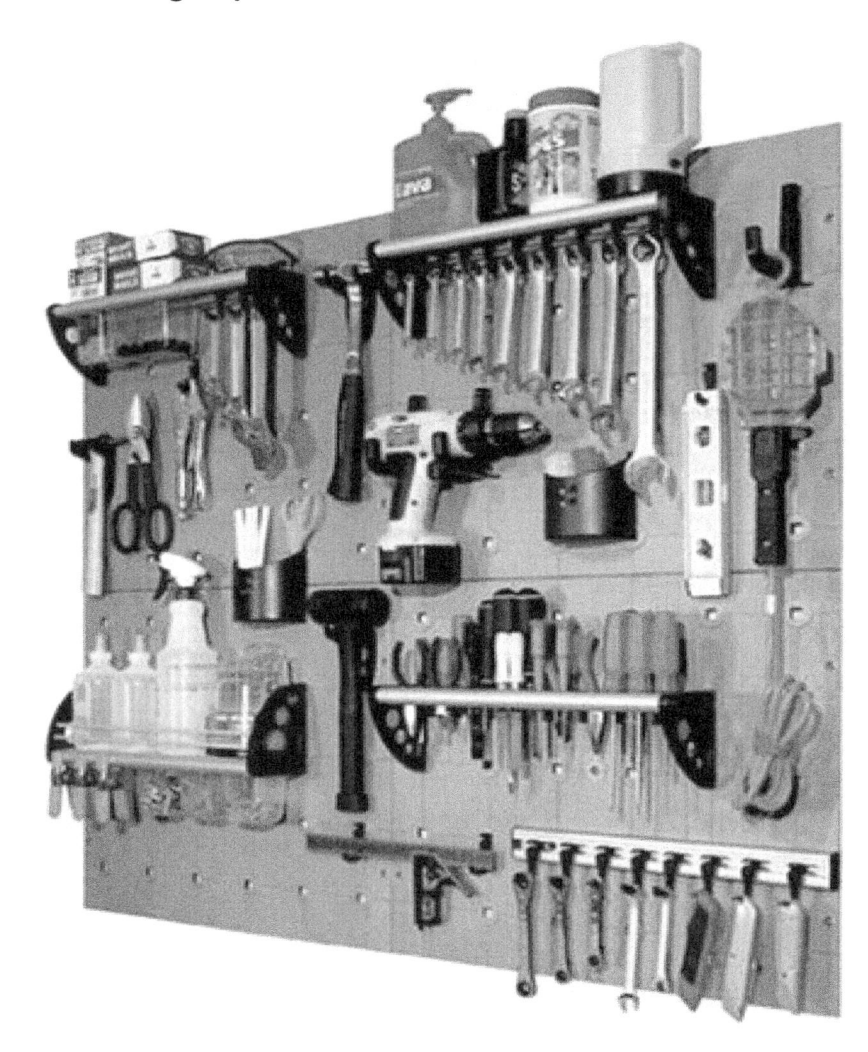

Storage of equipment is entirely up to your own personal style. Some people are so messy, and they leave stuff piled around them. They simply recall that on the router table, they left the moisture meter. Think about your organizational system, though. You will want to build cabinets or open shelves. In Mason jars, several woodworkers show fasteners that curl onto lids that have been nailed to an overhead board. Others have spent so many hours pulling fasteners out of Mason jars' shattered remnants and do not like the strategy. If you use a pegboard over your workbench for hand tools, remember to create the workbench narrow enough to reach the pegboard. The remedy for your hand tool storage, and a tackle box for fasteners, could be a rolling mechanic's toolbox. For the many pieces that accompany woodworking, some have hardware store-style bins. However, when you want to arrange your equipment and accessories, note that when you can find all your tools, your time on task is saved. When you have easy access to it, it's even easier to take care of expensive equipment. And it can save you a trip to the hardware store by having your fasteners sorted and easily accessible.

3.6 Power Tools every woodworker should have

Technically, a power tool is something that needs electrical power to work. We will discuss the simplest and modest tools.

The Bench Grinder

Have a decent bench grinder. You can even make a stand for this and keep this in the corner. It does not have to be in the way. Yet you'll be shocked by how much bench grinder you're going to use. You have to keep the sharpness of all your chisels and keep burrs off screwdrivers, too. The grinder doesn't cost too much, and when you have dull tools, time and money this saves you can be paying for itself in no time.

The Circular Saw

One of the most useful tools you can buy is a decent circular saw. Many individuals believe that a circular saw is a carpentry tool. However, they're just as precise as any of the tables saw, combined with correct clamping of the materials. Plus, for things that you might never try with the table saw, you should use a circular saw. Setting up a pair of the sawhorses and taking out the circular saw for cutting a sheet of the plywood or the MDF makes a lot of sense than having to walk around in the shop to cut them on the table saw. The first power tool in the shop should be a high-quality circular saw. There will be choices for how many teeth-per inches, or the TPI, you need on all your saws. You want to decide what you are looking for in a cut to make your decision. Saw blades with a lot of teeth can make cuts that are smoother. You run the risk of your wood being burnt, though. It is because a well-toothed saw works around the stock more slowly. As the holes between the teeth are narrower, it also doesn't clean sawdust out of the cut as easily. These holes are called the gullets, and on well-toothed saws, on a wide-toothed saw, several small gullets retain more sawdust than bigger gullets.

You should hold a set of blades for your saws, as a common rule of the thumb. With a 40-tooth saw blade, the circular saw and table saw, too, can make uneven cuts. With an 80-toothed saw blade, plywood and more laminated materials can work perfectly. The moisture content of your stock may be inaccurate if you know that blades of saws are accurate, but you are still having trouble cutting what you might want. Wood with a degree of moisture content that is very high for the region can "feather" when it is cut, nevertheless of blades' size or sharpness. When you cut wood that is very dry, it will crack and split. Use your moisture meter to verify the moisture content levels of your stock if this seems like no problem what you do for your saws. You still won't get satisfactory cuts.

The Power Drill

A power drill is the next tool of power that you can buy. Most people swear through cordless drills today, but they are more expensive, and they can't do anything an electric drill could do—where the word "power" comes in. They're not as costly as power drills, and they're further powerful than the cordless drills that have the place in the shop. The steady power of corded drills makes it a better instrument for prolonged use, particularly when big bits, like paddle bits, are used.

With two speeds to be choosing from, most power drills are variable speed. When you choose a power drill, you choose the wood chunk size you need 3x8 " or 1/2". The amount of bit you'll use will be determined by this. "You may want the 1/2" drill if you consider the need for greater drill bits, including for lag bars used in the decking. They've got more power as well. Usually, whether use chuck (keyless) or not, all chucks accommodate the smallest diameter. Few people swear through keyless chucks, and others know that they loosen on occasion.

The Sabre Saw

There should be a sabre saw for every woodworker. Sometimes referred to as jigsaw, it'll enable you to cut curves and patterns. Instead of a battery-operated one, you would definitely require an electric one, but battery-powered sabre saws work well on the thin material only with limited use. There's one you must find that would fit your hand. Very little, and you can't grip it; very large, and you cannot handle it. You will require a band saw for thicker materials.

The Palm Sander

For any woodworker's collection of power tools, a decent palm sander is essential. A 1/4 of a sheet of sanding paper can be used for the palm sander, which is thin enough for getting into tight positions. You must be careful, though, not to use the sand patterns, with a palm sander, in your finished job. In circular patterns, or back and forth, they normally move. They will leave swirls and lines in the wood that appear once it's stained; anyway, just be careful to keep this moving around the surface you're sanding so that you do not want sand grooves in the wood.

The Random Orbital Sander

Orbital sander (random) is basically a step upward from palm sander, "little brother" variant. Hook and loop (Velcro) are used by the random orbital sander to fasten sanding discs to the sanding pad. The erratic motion of the disc helps to stop the wood's sanding patterns. With this tool, the key precaution is to ensure that hardware supply stores have discs of each grit in stock. Otherwise, you're going to get a sander that you can't use because sanding pads can't be found with it.

The Table Saw

So now, in your woodworking shop, we'd start getting into the first lasting fixture: table saw. Table saws will, of course, be loaded into the bed of your vehicle because they are technically portable. However, the table saw isn't one that you could pick up and go to the worksite with one hand. A table saw is going to be the shop's workhorse, so buy a decent one. You're going to need it to miter, rip, mold, groove, square, and join, so it's important to get a decent saw that fits your needs. To endure the abuse, it would bear, the work surface must be of heavy-duty. Then to lift and lower the saw blade quickly, look for the handle. It should have another handle so the blade angle can be changed. See if there are ties to make that part simpler for dust collectors, too. You'll want to provide enough strength to the table saw to slice through the hardwood and make the deep cuts. Look at the amps and horsepower once more. The motor should begin and run smoothly with little or no vibration. Making sure it's blade guard and that it is easier to hit the on/off button. Power switch's paddle these days that, if you require an emergency shutdown, is easy to press with your knee. The blades are in the same group as hand saws on your table saw: rip and crosscut. There are large gullets on rip blades. For either tooth, on opposite sides, crosscut blades have kerf or additional cutting chisels. This produces a surface of very fine cut. A rip blade is designed for cutting when you rip stock with the grain of the wood. It is possible to cut crosscut blades either with it or against the grain. Combination blades are the most widely bought blades, varying from twenty-four TPI to eighty TPI.

The Jig and Dado

If you have the entire spectrum of dados and jigs to use for it, the table saw is much more flexible. Jigs and their usage for tendons, tapering, panel-cutting, and several other uses were listed earlier in this list. Two blades with a set of wood chippers in between are a stacked dado. This is used to break grooves or removing large stock pieces. Although the chipper eliminates much of the material between the saw blades, the saw blades make the side of the groove straight. To get wider cuts, you should change the width of the chippers. For this, you should even use a wobble saw, but it wobbles and vibrates the table saw, not cutting a flat edge.

The Compound Miter Saw

You do have a Tenon saw with a miter box, so you'll need a compound miter saw if you venture into the crown molding and other ventures like that. For those beveled cuts and miters, you could have used your circular saw. For those hybrid cuts, though, nothing beats the accuracy of a decent compound miter saw. It is possible to set a miter saw to bevel up to 45 degrees and to trim in both directions at a 60-degree angle. It should be easy to read and clearly labeled with the miter gauge on the saw. Hard stops, such as 0, 15, 22.5, 30, and 45, should occur at each major stage. On all sides, those degrees should be avoided. Not just that, but at any angle, you should be able to lock the saw.

The bevel on the saw is the capacity to tilt the saw, thus the term, to compound the cut. This gives you the opportunity to use one break to cut two angles. If you intend to cut 6" wood, you will need a 10" saw blade. The 12" blade is good, but few individuals really need the extra dimension. Even if they have it, they appreciate it. For most woodworkers, 8" blades are far too short.

You will find compound miter saws that act as a radial arm saw with a sliding arm, but they're pretty costly.

The Router

Each woodworker ought to have a router. You will form the edges of your work with the router. With the different parts available, the number of shapes is infinite. A stationary base router can do about everything you need if you are a novice. This will start and finish the cut at the same depth you have set before the cut is made. You should plunge the bit into the wood with a plunge router, cut, and raise it back up. You can use your stationary router in a router table and make long cuts with ease using a fence. To use the rip fence and feather boards, some woodworkers also adapt their table saw to accept a stationary router. For hardwoods, you can get a router with at least 2 HP or it will be underpowered. Because broad bits need to run at slower rates, it requires variable speeds. If you don't have a router with a variable speed, you should burn the bits. You can burn the hardwoods, too, if you can't slow down the router's pace.

The Band Saw

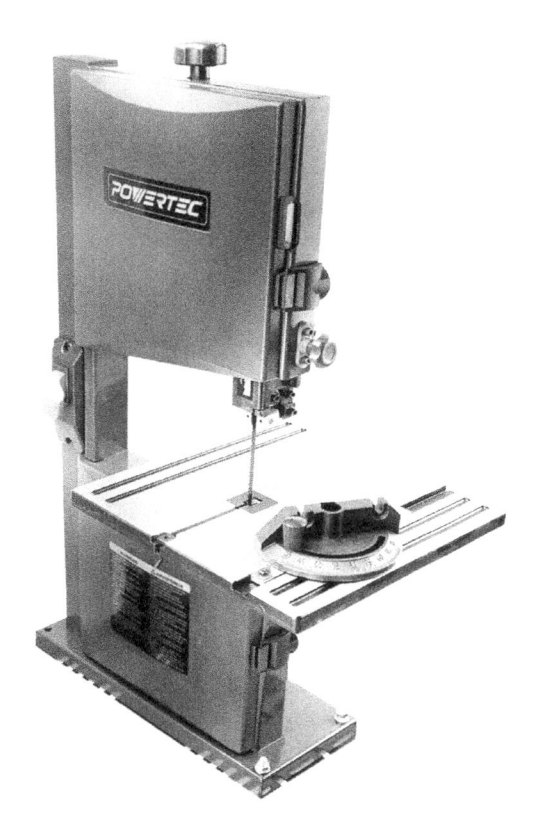

For cutting precise shapes and curves, you simply can't beat a band saw. Although, what many woodworkers do not know is that when cutting rabbets and tendons, the band saw a strong friend. With a band saw, you can even rip tiny bits of wood and make your laminate strips. You can attach free-standing models to a workbench or a dedicated stand or cabinet, band saws, and table mount models. Typically, the free-standing versions are heavier, more durable saws, and have more functionality. They have bigger engines as well. For your band saw, you'll want to look at two things: the width of the cut and the throat. The cutting depth is the width of the blade between the cutting plate and the upper guides. The thickness of the stock you will cut will be determined by this. However, several saws can have risers added to make it easier to cut heavier materials, but with the help of a riser, you can go from 6 to 12 inches. The gap from the saw blade to the saw's back frame is the throat. A cabinet band saw will have a deeper throat, usually about 18", whereas 12" to 14" throats are available for the bench versions. The width of stock you will cut will be determined by this. When you see data that refers to a 12-inch band saw, it refers to the throat.

The Radial Arm Saw

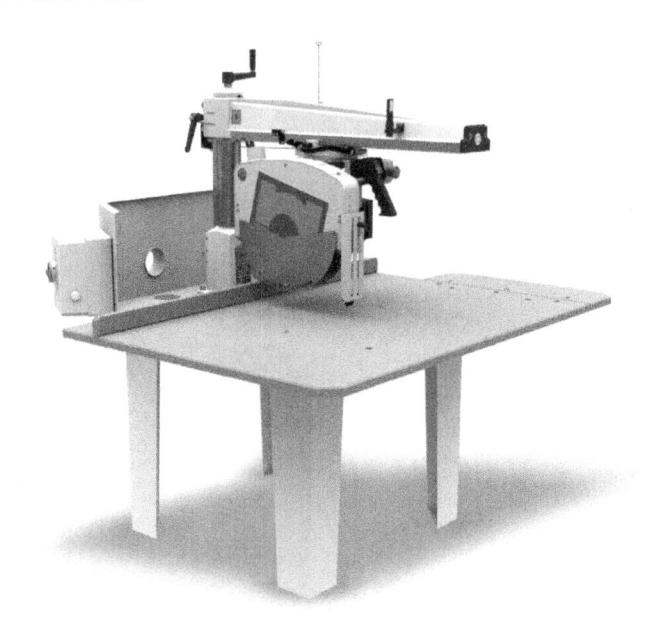

The saw for the radial arm is costly, heavy, and bulky. And, for those who possess one, it is indispensable. Typically, the radial arm saw is used to execute crosscuts. You can use it, though, for bevels and miters, rabbets, moldings, and even as a guide for the router. Like a compound miter saw and a table saw, it will do the same tasks. However, it's a bit more difficult to use in these capacities. It's sort of a tradeoff; with the more extravagant price, you get a multi-purpose saw, but it would be a bit harder to use than saws made exclusively for such purposes.

You would transfer the saw, rather than the stuff, with a radial arm saw. With this screw, the width of the throat can make a difference. Your set-up will decide the success of your work. Carefully put up the fence, and make sure that your stock is snug against it. Switch on the saw then, and let the blade get up to full speed before you begin to drag it towards you.

The Surface Planer

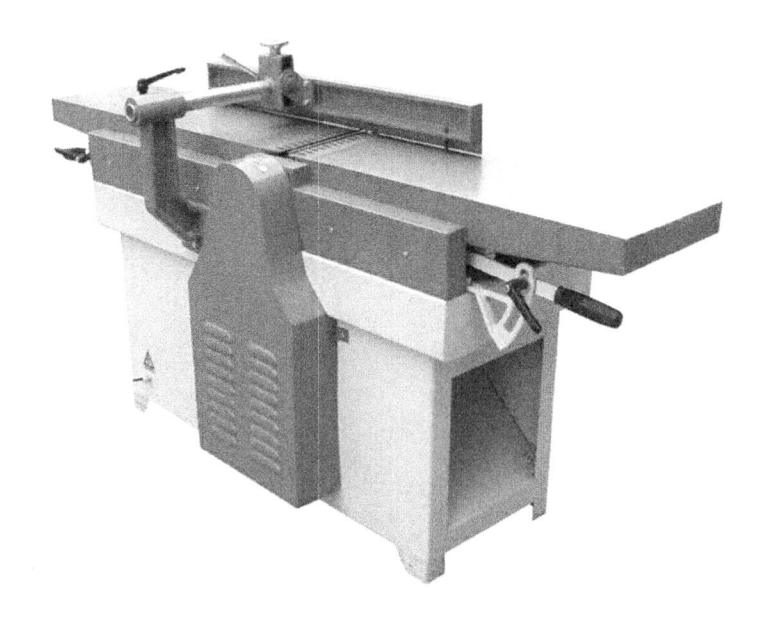

For the diligent woodworkers over the years who have patiently and skillfully designed their stock by hand to get the right thickness, the surface planer is the high-tech solution. The time-saving surface glider makes the world a lot better. There is a table on which you feed your stock to the planer. This table is between 10" and 14", so you can give the full stock width through it. When it is fed in, a series of blades rotates, cutting the wood.

With a crank, you adjust the cut's depth, usually on one end of the planer. It looks like the wheel on a sewing machine. Most planers can plane your stock down 6 inches, but you need to do this in small increments.

The Jointer

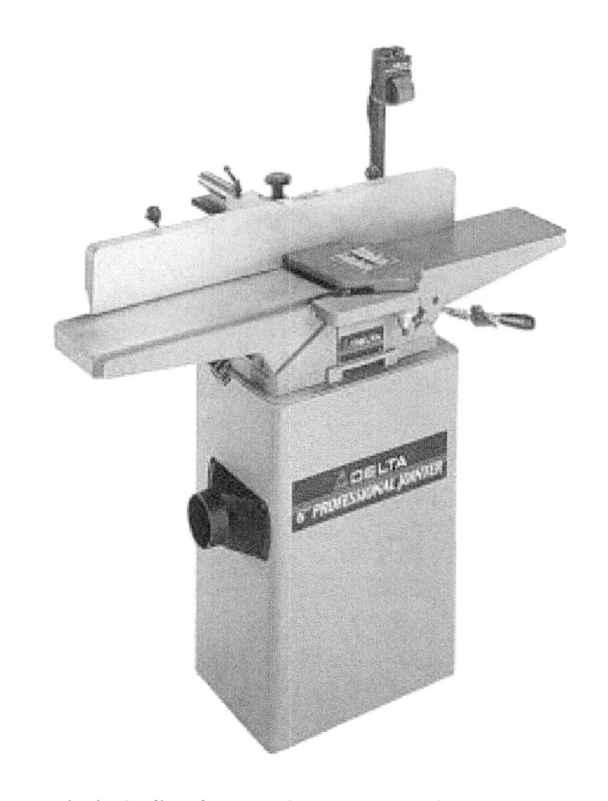

The most effective and detailed way to guarantee square edges is the jointer. It will also yield smooth surfaces that will not move through the surface planer. The jointer uses a cutter head that rotates at high RPM rather than using a saw blade. It is placed between two tables. Depending on how many you want to withdraw from your stock, the in-feed table is normally at a lower height. The out-feed table, which protects the board when it is sliced, is at the same height as the cutting point. To better have detailed splits, there should also be a barrier.

To do the woodworking, you would require a flat edge, and a flat edge can be cut on your stock by the jointer. For instance, if you have a 2–4 with a roughed-up edge, you can put it on the jointer, rough side down, against the fence. Move the 2–4 over the jointer knives with a push handle, and it can cut down the rough areas of the edge. To have a completely smooth surface, you have to make many passes. Not only can this help you with safer cuts, but it will spare your engine and knives from wear and tear. Also, mind to still encourage the blades before you start cutting to get up to full speed.

The Safety Equipment

You should save irreplaceable parts of the surveillance systems you use. Fingers don't grow back, so use feather boards, push sticks, and use tools as directed at all times. When you feed material into machines, you should still have the proper backup and keep the pressure applied to the right sections of the stock, as in your instruction manuals. Your hearing and vision are similarly irreplaceable, so wear safety glasses at all times. You buy them with protective lenses while you wear prescription lenses, making it easier to cover your eyes when you're working. Ordinary glasses are not safety lenses, and if a projectile strikes them, they can shatter, causing further damage.

CHAPTER 4:

Woodworking Projects

To take on one of these outdoor woodworking projects as beginners, you don't need to be an expert woodworker or own professional tools. Each of the simple projects included here comes with successful tips. Check out all these useful and attractive projects you can build! The best thing is they do not require a full workshop and years of training in woodworking, only a few basic devices, and few old-fashioned grease elbows.

1. Cantilever End Table

Tools You Need

- Brad nail gun of 16 inch
- Screws
- Driver/drill
- Miter Saw
- Table Saw

Materials You Need

- Plain screws of 1–1/4"
- Board of 1x2
- 1x3 of 2-in. sixteen-gauge Brad Nails
- 3-in. of bolts
- Around 3/4-in. plywood
- Painter's tape
- Wooden glue

Tech Art

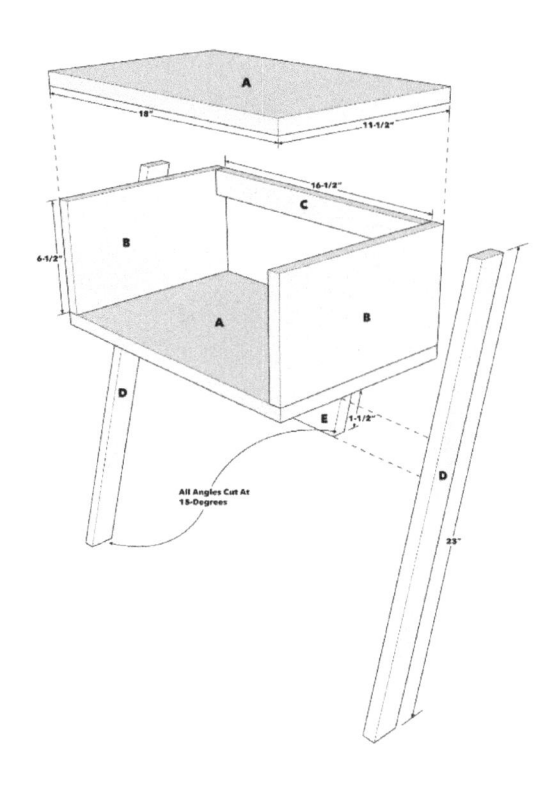

Cutting list

Key	Qty	Material	Dimensions	Part
A	2	3/4" Plywood	3/4" x 11-1/2" x 18"	Box top & bottom
B	2	3/4" Plywood	3/4" x 11-1/2" x 6-1/2"	Box sides
C	1	1x2 Pine	3/4" x 1-1/2" x 16-1/2"	Nailer strip
D	2	1x2 Pine	3/4" x 1-1/2" x 23"	Legs
E	1	1x3 Pine	3/4" x 1-1/2" x 18"	Bottom Base

Step by Step Project

1. **Mill components to fit**

For the proportions of the top and bottom of the box (A), box sides (B), and the nail strips, consider the cutting list (C). Cut angles to 15 degrees at the edges of the 1x2 wooden legs (D). The bottom brace (E) is cut to length, and all ends are twisted on the table saw for about 15 degrees. 1–1/2 in. is the completed width.

2. **Organize the box**

Clamp and tighten the edges of the box sides with 2-in. brad nails to the top and bottom of the box (A). Check the square. Glue, clamp, and attach the nail string (C) with 2-inch brad nails to the back edge of the box. Fill every hole with wood filler, and afterward, sand seamlessly.

3. **Prime, polish, and finish**

Prime the box and paint it. You may need a coat of more than one. Stain and let the legs or bottom brace dry.

4. Fasten the legs

End up making a 4-in. from the lower end of the front of the box. Fasten the legs in position so that the legs' angles are swish with the box's top and integrate with the stamp you have made.

Tape to the legs (D). Between the bits of tape, place a shovel in the pilot holes for the legs. Fasten the legs in position, then shovel the pilot holes from within the box into them. For the screw heads, countersink and tighten the legs with 1–1/4 inch screws.

5. Connect the brace from the edge

Use 2-in. brad nails to glue, clamp, and attach the lower support to the legs. Place the front side of the legs with the front of the bottom support and the curved edge with the bottom of the case.

2. Hexagonal Shelves

Tools You Need

- Table Saw

Materials you need

- 4' of 2x6 wood (one shelf)
- Painter's tape
- Wooden glue

Step by Step Project

1. Through the board, crosscut angle

In this design, a little amount of math is involved. There are inner angles of 120 ° in a curved hexagon, part of which would be 60 degrees. It has a corresponding angle of 30 degrees. This is the point at which you need to set the saw. If the saw can be fixed to 30 degrees, it will be very convenient to use a miter saw. For an initial perspective, crosscut one of the edges of the board.

2. Put up a halt and continue the cuts

To get clear cuts, mount a stop at 7 inches alongside the miter gauge with a screw (or mount the block to the transitory fence). To get all the components for the design, cut six boards.

3. Tape the boards together

It can be surprisingly complicated and laborious to fasten the boards along with conventional clamps. In these situations, it is simple to erase and does not significantly impact the wood, but retains well enough to accomplish the job. With the pointy end grains touching, glue the boards together. To ensure the angles are good, close up the shelf, and it fits around each other.

4. Glue the boards together

Glue the boards with the final grain, making sure the glue is spread all the way to the corners. With a couple of final pieces of tape, flip the structure up and protect it. Let it dry to your preference and add the finish. You might use wood filler to plug holes if you have any handy, or there are several other ways to achieve the same thing with components already in the workshop.

3. Wooden Key Hanger

Tools You Need

- The 18-Gauge Brad Nail Gun
- Screws
- Miter saw
- Sander/Planer
- Table Saw

Materials You Need

- 1-1/2-in. brad nails of 18-gauge
- Wood, recycled
- Wooden glue

Tech Art

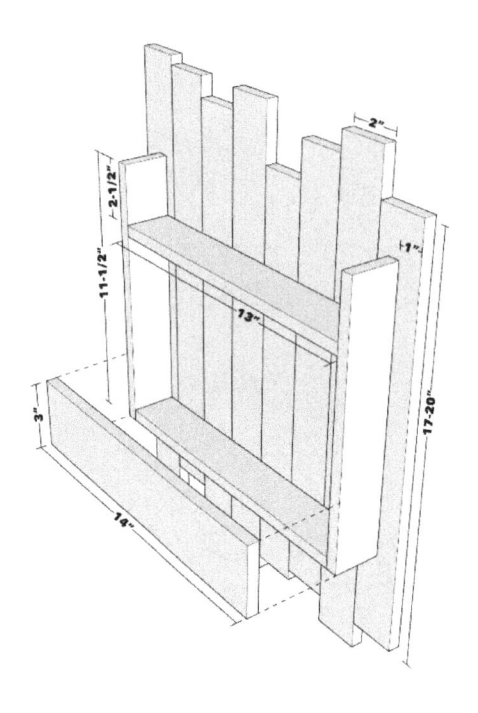

Cutting List

Key	Qty	Material	Dimensions	Part
A	8	Reclaimed Wood	(Variable) x 2" x 17-20"	Back Boards
B	1	Reclaimed Wood	(Variable) x 3" x 14"	Front Board
C	2	Reclaimed Wood	(Variable) x 2" x 11-1/2"	Vertical Pieces
D	2	Reclaimed Wood	(Variable) x 2" x 13"	Shelves

Step by Step Projects

1. **Line up the edges**

Mostly, the recycled wood is far from the square. Fix it by lining up the boards on the saw of the bench. Take the edges off as few as possible.

2. **Cut boards to fit**

To cut all of the boards but one to 2 inches, use a table saw. For the front of the hanger, knock the very last board down to 3 inches.

3. Split boards to size

To 11–1/2 in. and twice more to 13 inches on the miter saw, crosscut two of the 2-in. boards. Split the remainder of the panels between 17 inches or 20 inches to varying lengths.

4. Scribe and Split the Front Board

Deride up the main hanger and position the 3-inch board where it'll be placed on the panel—scribe for a precise calculation of the board. Cut the 3-inch board to that length on the miter saw.

5. **Organize the Hanger's Front**

Use glue as well as 18-gauge 1–1/2 inch brad nails to gather the front of the hanger. The top shelf of the longitudinal boards is 2–1/2 inches from the top. You can quickly make this venture with 1–1/2 inch if you're not using an 18-gauge brad nail gun: building screws, pilot gaps, and a drill.

6. **Plane the rear panels**

Plane to make a flat back on one hand of the discrete length boards. Dust the boards with close to zero sandpaper to have the boards flat if you don't have a glider.

7. Glue the Rear Boards Up

In whichever configuration you want, glue and attach the eight discrete boards; just don't mitigate the boards further than 1 inch, or the front framework won't match appropriately.

8. Design completion

On each side of the assembly, glue and nail the front structure to the rear with a 1-inch relief. If you do not have a Brad nail gun, use a drill and screws.

4. Portable Laptop Stand

Tools You Need

- 1/2-in. Bit of Spade
- Drill
- Hammer
- Jigsaw
- A printer
- Punch

Materials You Need

- Dowel, 1/2-in.
- 1/2-in. of plywood

Cutting List

Key	Qty	Material	Dimensions	Part
A	2	1/2" Plywood	1/2" x 6" x 10"	Supports
B	1	1/2" Dowel	1/2" x 10"	Dowel

Step by Step Project

1. Split out the support

Cover the plywood workspace with masking tape. Break the prototype printed out and nail it with the plywood. Track the prototype around and identify the position of the dowel hole with a middle punch. Using the jigsaw, clamp the panel to the worktable and take out the supports. The close radius can be cut quickly with a 1/8-in. knife. To build the second support, repeat this stage. Cut the dowel to a length of 1/2-in.

2. Dustup to size

Drop the masking tape on the worktable or in your position, then attach the supports together—sand off all of the saw markings, beginning with 60-grit sandpaper. Sanding with the clamped sections means that they will remain the same. Up to 180 or 220-grit, work your way. To get through the narrow radius, tie sandpaper across a slice of the remaining dowel.

3. Drill the holes

Fasten the support to your worktable, with a ritualistic board beneath with a 1/2-in. spade bit, and drill a hole between the two supports. Feel free to add the finish of your preference.

Chapter 5:

Tips for Starting the Woodworking

Given that you have a basic plan, follow the tips to set yourself up for success just as you start your woodworking journey.

Start with What You Have

Typically, everybody has several tools or/and wood lying nearby. Find a project that you can complete with only what you have already on hand. It can save you time, make a trip to the supermarket, help you de-clutter and take advantage of what you have.

Buy Tools You Will Use Anyway

Instead of winding up with a workshop full of big powerful tools to trade or store, stay with small hand-held equipment and electric equipment that can come in convenient even though you don't continue with a woodworking hobby.

Start with Hand Tools before Power Tools

As already stated, it's maybe wise to start a woodworking voyage with the simplest hand tools. This can make tasks a little longer. However, you'll save resources and energy, so when you're studying, you'll be capable of focusing your time on cuts a little more. Even if you figure out that you don't like woodworking, you've got only a handful of spare hand tools that you could need for anything else.

Initially Invest in Small Power Tools

Start with power hand tools when you're ready for moving into power tools beforehand, moving on to big stationary tools. Once you are confident and genuinely passionate about woodworking, table saws are an excellent device and are usually called the woodshop cornerstone.

Invest in Quality for Heavily Used Tools

If you find a tool you often use, don't be frightened to participate in truly great quality items. Heavy usage of the tool means even the slight increase in the quality and user-friendliness can deliver a much better return in time and effort saved.

Buy Tools and Supplies as and when Required

Rather than running out and maxing out the credit cards in different materials, supplies, and tools, start with one simple project and buy the items needed for that project alone. Then when you go on to some other project, purchase the things required for the one.

Measure Twice, Cut Once

The significance of checking twice the measurements really can't be stressed enough. Having to begin over on an almost finished item because this was cut very small can be a real pain. It is especially relevant for the project where you just have a small number of wood or complex-piece projects. Starting in those cases can be tremendously time-consuming, if possible. So begin right by checking measurements twice habitually, and you can spare yourself real pain in the head later on.

Label Your Cut Parts as You Cut Them

When you do more complex tasks, you will get into cases where you create numerous cuts for various sections, only to discover that you have messed up the separate pieces and scraps from cuts. You then have to measure everything again to sort out what's what. To label/mark your parts as you slit them is a good solution. If you are using a lead pencil (soft), you may easily sand the label off if necessary. If you love puzzles, you may ignore this tip.

Cut Pieces a Little Larger

To account for cutting, sanding errors, and other potential problems, cutting project pieces slightly greater than the required size is generally a good practice, particularly for a beginner. Remember, removing more material is much easier than adding once it's been removed.

Keep the Smallest Scraps of Wood

It is not surprising that very tiny pieces of wood could create jigs, inlays, caps, etc. Setting aside a place where tiny pieces of wood can be kept is a useful idea. This may be a big bin or crate or any part of your woodworking/shop room.

But feel free to rid yourself of little tiny scraps. Assuming wood is unprocessed, mulch, fire starter, or different uses can be workable options for the leftover wood.

Keep Your Work Area Clean and Organized

Built-up scattered wooden chips, wood dust, unsystematic tools, etc., could all turn into major wood-shop problems. Wood dust may get all over, ruin the finishes, and even causes health problems. Wood chips could be caught between the things and cuts, and joint fittings can be messed up. Jumbled tools may be difficult to locate while you want them fast or lost completely over extended periods.

Conclusion

Some things are essential to know before starting woodworking. These are essential both for beginners and experienced woodworkers. Woodworking can be an entertaining activity where you can express yourself creatively and work with your hands. Woodworking can be an extremely rewarding hobby. It can be productive, even profitable while being relaxing and meditative at the same time. With a very reasonable investment of time and money, you would be surprised at the quality of what you can produce.

Moreover, using simple and affordable tools, wood can be cut and shaped, making it a comparatively low investment-based hobby. Whether you're looking for furniture construction, tackling some of the home improvement projects, or building little objects such as jewelry boxes, you must know that woodworking requires only a small number of tools and resources. Usually, beforehand making any of the cuts, most of the woodworking projects require you to measure and mark your cuts out on the wood. Tape measure, carpenter's pencil, and a mix square are important devices for such jobs. Cutting wood is, of course, the backbone of woodworking. A circular hand saw is an essential power tool for creating straight cuts. Similarly, the jigsaw is perfect for creating rounded cuts. Hand backsaw acts as a good substitute for power.

You'll also need to sculpt the wood by making beveled edges or delicate molding to generate woodworking projects having sleek, finished looks. The essential wood shaping tools include some block plane that will help you make simple beveled edges and a router that can be equipped with a range of bits to help you build more complex designs. Screws, nails, and glue are necessary as they help to assemble your projects in woodworking. For drilling holes, a cordless drill is often essential, while the screwdriver, hammer, and clamps are very useful. You can also opt for a 1-handed clamp bar for your first clamp. The most straightforward approach when joining the wood is the butt joint, within which you may simply butt one panel's end grain against another. This joint may be secured for a clean look using glue or sometimes with screws to have a more rugged and less good-looking finish. Biscuit joiner's some power tool which cuts into each part of wood a narrow groove that can be joined easily. You may then fit little wood chips known as "biscuits," which give you additional stability for glued join in these grooves. Another method to improve the adhesion's surface area is to carve a groove into one piece of timber. These grooves permit the 2nd piece of timber to contact the 1st piece along many surfaces. Dadoes, Rabbits, and grooves are three kinds of this combination, called according to the cut's inclination against the wood's grain. Of course, the very important woodworking joints are the dovetail, the mortise, and Tenon in it; the two pieces of wood interconnect with each other. These joints' elegance and strength are unparalleled. Applying boiled linseed oil and furniture wax is the most mistake-proof method to finish timber designs. These polishes may be applied using cotton rags, thus eliminating any risk of brush lashes or further defects. For surfaces that take on more abuse, such as a table in the dining room, you will desire a finish that cures a protective hard layer. Polyurethane is a standard product, especially for this kind of finish. It may be applied with a foam brush or bristle brush of high quality. There are several other methods to finish the timber, each with its benefits, disadvantages, and appearances. Wood oils, lacquers, paints, teak oil, varnishes, and Danish oils are all popular choices in your woodworking projects to produce durable, attractive finishes. You have to create a simple woodworking setup, know how to read a tape measure, develop an understanding of wood and related species' dimensions, and learn how to use woodworking tools and tools to produce your woodworking projects.

Made in United States
North Haven, CT
26 November 2021